Everyone knows about Mary's visit from the Angel Gabriel, Jesus's somewhat eccentric birth next door to that famous one-star inn (now the Bethlehem Happy Eater), and all his miraculous exploits leading to his inspiring death, but have you ever wondered what Jesus got up to in all those years that are *not* reported in the Bible? There's a huge void between the time when he went missing, aged twelve, for three days (only to be found chatting up rabbis in the synagogue), and the triumphant come-back tour in his late twenties.

Did he do well at school for instance? Come to that, did he even go to school? If he did, what was his favourite subject? Was he a real goody-goody and teacher's pet like we are led to believe? Or was he a sort of embryonic Paul Daniels (perish the thought), or Tommy Cooper, always practising tricks (before learning the art of the miracle), on his unsuspecting mates?

Come to that, who were his mates? Perhaps he had his own gang – kind of junior-league disciples. Was he into girls, or was he a late developer?

These and many other mysteries of Jesus's teenage years will be revealed in the following long-lost, but truly fascinating, diaries of the boy who was to become the most famous person ever.

John Farman

JESUS
THE TEENAGE YEARS

By the same author:

The Very Bloody History of Britain
The Very Bloody History of Britain 1945 to Now

John Farman

JESUS THE TEENAGE YEARS

The Bodley Head
London

1 3 5 7 9 10 8 6 4 2

Copyright © John Farman 1995

John Farman has asserted his right under the
Copyright, Designs and Patents Act, 1988, to be
identified as the author and illustrator of this work

First published in the United Kingdom 1995
by the Bodley Head Children's Books
Random House, 20 Vauxhall Bridge Road,
London SW1V 2SA

Random House Australia (Pty) Limited
20 Alfred Street, Milsons Point, Sydney
New South Wales 2061, Australia

Random House New Zealand Limited
18 Poland Road, Glenfield
Auckland 10, New Zealand

Random House South Africa (Pty) Limited
PO Box 337, Bergvlei 2012, South Africa

Random House UK Limited Reg. No. 954009

A CIP catalogue record for this book is
available from the British Library

ISBN 0 370 32331 9

Phototypeset by Intype, London

Printed in Great Britain by
Mackays of Chatham PLC, Chatham, Kent

Contents

The Diary

Have you ever heard of *The Dead Sea Scrolls?* (Found in all good history books!) These ancient documents, discovered at Wadi al-Marabbah'ah, up Palestine way, in 1947, are the greatest proof ever of the existence of the late, great, Jesus of Nazareth.

Have you ever heard of Ebenezer Farman, my great uncle (deceased – not mentioned in *any* history book)? I expect not. He was a shadowy 'hanger-on'; a kind of archaeological groupie, travelling the world, ferreting around under all the newly discovered sites immediately after the main treasures had been whipped away and the other 'proper' archaeologists had gone for a well-earned pint.

Under where the most important scrolls were found, old Ebenezer dug up a much smaller 'scroll-ette' which left him, even after many years, rather puzzled. It appeared to be some sort of diary, though whose it actually was, he had no idea. All he'd been able to decipher from the ancient script was the word Jesus. The trouble was that in those days Jesuses were two a-penny (like Johns in the nineteen forties) so he was never quite sure if it was the Jesus of bible fame – or not.

1

Being the fine scholar what I am (O level Woodwork – Grade C), I have been able to translate large chunks of the diary from the Aramaic language (which Jesus would have spoken) and am about to let you in on it. Before we kick off, however, let me briefly put you in the picture as to what was going on up Galilee way (where our Jesus lived).

Galilee was still a rather insignificant province in a largely godforsaken little backwater of the Roman Empire, which was currently being ruled by their brand new emperor, Tiberius. It had been divided up between the three sons of bad King Herod (the boy-killer), who were answerable in turn to the Romans, who were surfing on the crest of their world power.

The good folk of Israel, however, were continually on the look-out for a new warrior king (or Messiah), from the line of David, who would eventually show their Roman overlords where to get off. Our hero actually fitted the bill quite well, as his family could be traced through his dad Joseph – his dad Heli – his dad Matthat – his dad Levi and so on and so on, right back to David. David, in turn, could be tracked right back through hundreds more dads to your actual Adam, who was the first guy that God made (and who mated with Eve).

Just to put the whole caboodle into its historical context, it might be worth noting that Jesus lived only a few years before those wretched Romans poured onto the English beaches near Margate (at which point lesser legions would have turned back!), marched up the A2, and invented London in AD 43. During

2

Jesus's severely curtailed lifetime, the Romans invented soap, the Turks invented delight and the very clever Chinese invented plactically everything else (including take-aways).

Important Note

Before we dive into the diary, there's something you really ought to know. After the somewhat weird circumstances surrounding the birth of their first-born (angels, wise men, shepherds), Mary and Joseph decided that, in order for him to have a normal childhood and adolescence, they wouldn't let him in on the plot until the end of his teenage years. Jesus, therefore, had no idea that he was the son of God, or what the old chap had in store for him. Please read on . . .

Jesus Comes of Age

25th December 9 AD*

Dear Diary

Yippee, I'm a teenager at long last!
I awoke this morning expecting
to feel different. Verily, for the last
year I dreamt of my thirteenth birthday
and my Bar Mitzvah, for it is the day
that we Jewish boys traditionally
get promoted from childhood to
adulthood. No more boring grown-ups
sending me to bed at an early hour;
no one bending my ear that my opinions
are no good because I'm a mere kid;
no one forcing me to sit with the
youngsters at dreary birthday parties or celebrations; and, just
think, no silly prat patting me patronisingly on the head and telling
me that, verily, one day I might be able to get my head round what
he or she talketh about. Just as I was lying back revelling in these
thoughts, my mother burst upon me.

'And what time dost thou call this, idle boy? Come down this
minute and have your cornflakes; and make sure you cleaneth your
teeth and have a good wash – especially behind those ears.' She
then put her head into her hands, 'Dear Lord, kids today!' she
added despairingly.

---

* You might wonder why the date starts on 9 AD instead of 13 AD. Apparently, in the 6th century, when they were trying to invent the calendar that we use today, someone made an almighty cock-up with his sums and recorded our hero's birth four years too early. By the time they discovered the mistake, it was too late to do anything about it.

4

Blimey, I thought, this is a fine start to grown-updom. The old lady treateth me like a nipper still. When I got downstairs I launched into her.

'Mother dear, I supposeth not that you happen to recall what day it is?'

"Course I do, it's Monday – washing day and I'm well behind. Now break your fast and get out of my way. How expecteth thou that I should run this household with kids hanging upon my apron strings all day?'

Kids! Who was she calling a kid? Damn cheek. I was well angry, but also somewhat crestfallen. Usually my family made quite a big deal of birthdays; everybody treating you nicely (for once), loads of presents and, generally, some sort of a 'do' in the evening. I was well miffed, therefore, that she seemed to have forgotten.

'Isn't there anything rather special about today, Ma?' I enquired casually, 'anything that separateth it from any other Monday in the year?'

Mother stopped what she was doing and rubbed her chin.

'Well, let me see. It's not your pa's and my wedding anniversary; no one's getting married; no one's coming to stay and no one seemeth to have passed away. No, I really can't think of anything. Why?'

'Well, doesn't thou remember something that happened thirteen years ago in Bethlehem,' I asked, beginning to feel a bit narked.

'Thirteen years ago? Now you're asking . . .' she pondered, strolling up and down the kitchen, hands upon hips. 'Forsooth, it's such a long time ago, I can't rightly recall. All I can remember was that terrible trek thy dad and I had to do when those blasted Romans suddenly decided to count up all the people they'd conquered. But apart from that I really. . . .'

'Oh come on, Ma! Don't you remember what arrived whilst you were there?'

I was becoming more and more cross and, verily, felt my colour rising. How dare she forget my birthday?

'Arrived? Hang on now thou comest to mention it, I do remember something. Oh yes – silly me! Your Uncle Jacob, the one that's a bit underwhelming in the brain department, turned up with his new, dreadful common wife and. . . .'

'MOTHER', I screamed. 'Don't you remember? It was my. . . .'

Suddenly the door burst assunder, and a host of voices yelled 'HAPPY BIRTHDAY!' Into the room tumbled my dad, Naomi (the big girl with the small moustache) from next door, and a gaggle of rowdy rellies and neighbours.

Mother fell upon her chair laughing as the small throng gathered round, patting me on the back and handing me gifts.

As the day progressed, Jesus met all his friends and acquaintances and was smothered in presents and congratulations. He was a nipper no longer. He called in at the synagogue and the old rabbis, who had always had a very soft-spot for him, greeted him warmly. They put on a special *Bar Mitzvah* service, with lots of pomp and circumstance, in which they welcomed our hero to adulthood and told him that he was now responsible for his own faith. . . .

Back home, Mary, Rachel and Rachel's mum prepared a huge feast for the evening while, out in the backyard, Joseph barbied a calf that had been fattened for months.

At around seven of the clock, the guests began to pitch up at our front door. They all, strangely enough, commented on a strange, bright star that seemed to be hanging about right over our house. Mum and Dad spent more time than most gazing upon it, and seemed to appear a touch edgy. Lo, at about eight o'clock, a small gang of shepherds turned up (sheep and all) saying they'd come for some sort of reunion, but seemed to clam up completely when I

introduced myself. I must admit I thought it a bit uncool that they'd
simply arrived at the door without an invite, but asked them in
anyway – they looked as if they could do with a good square meal
and a stiff drink. All throughout the feast, however, they kept giving
me funny, adoring looks and every now and again would fall upon
their knees in front of me. This began to get on my nerves, so I
told them that, though I appreciated their gratitude, there was no
need for all that nonsense. Crikey! If one couldn't share a meal,
said I, it would be a very poor show in-blinking-deed.

And it came to pass, at around ten o'clock, cousin Joab, who'd
spent most of the evening lounging outside our back gate snogging
the young Ehabson girl from three doors down, sauntered up looking
well pleased with himself.

'What hast thou been up to Joab, as if I didn't know?' I asked
inquisitively.

'Oh nothing much, Jeez. I've just shooed away some gatecrashers,'
he replied in his smuggest voice. 'Its bad enough having a host of
scruffy shepherds arriving uninvited – but commercial travellers!'

'Commercial travellers? What commmercial travellers? What were
they like?' I asked, not liking to see anyone turned away empty-
handed (or tummied!).

Mum and Dad looked more nervous than before.

'Well,' he said, 'there were three of them – real old, and riding upon
motheaten old camels. I thinketh someone must have told them
we were having some sort of fancy dress party 'cos they were all
dressed up as kings, with silly false beards and sparkly crowns.
Foreign looking they were.'

'What sayest you to them?' I asked, worried that he might have
been too rude.

'Well, they looked to be carrying various products which they
seemed to want me to look at. Blimey, I thought, I've been caught
like that in the past. Before you know where you are, they say you've
handled the goods so you've got to keep 'em. Actually, I don't think
they were too sure of the language, so I had to speak real slow.'

'So what didst you say to them,' I repeated.

'I simply told them that my auntie never buys nuffink at the door,
and that if they didn't get lost, I'd go and get my dad who'd soon
see 'em off.'

I rushed out to the front gate, but lo, the three peddlars were
just specks in the distance. Ah well, I thought, I suppose it was all
for the best. My mum's got enough brushes and pots and pans to
last her a lifetime.

7

Upstairs, Mary and Joseph had also watched nervously, as the three old men disappeared into the distance. They'd recognized them instantly as the same wise kings that they'd last met thirteen years ago, but were still anxious to keep the real truth from their very special son.

Jesus and Goliath

Jesus was a good lad at school. He worked conscientiously at his lessons (without being a swot), and was popular amongst *most* of his schoolmates. On open days, his teacher, Mrs Nathanson, always told Jesus's parents what a fine boy their son was but, on the down side, how he was given to daydreaming in lessons and seeming to be always at the centre of funny pranks and tricks (early miracles?). His favourite subject was RE, but although his knowledge of the Old Testament was nothing less than staggering for a lad of his age, she thought he was far too bright and intelligent to go into the church for a living. This pleased his mum no end, for despite all the fuss surrounding his less than normal birth, she'd always dreamed of him being a doctor or lawyer.

The only thing that clouded his fairly idyllic school days, was the way he was bullied by a couple of the older, more robust (in all but the brain department) boys. Also, because he was always seeming to help people; was fond of the scriptures; and could not be bothered to try in sport (as he didn't see the point), he was regarded by some as a bit of a sissy. There was one particular lad, Reuben, nicknamed Golly (short for Goliath) – on account of his being twice to three times the size of the other kids in his year – who seemed to have a personal vendetta against our hero. He certainly wasn't the brightest creature that ever walked God's earth, and therefore resented goody-goody (his words) Jesus's popularity, not only with the teacher, but particularly, and more importantly, with the girls.

9

8th February 10 AD

Dear Diary

Had a woeful day at school today. Gol...sorry Reuben hath been telling all the others that he's finally had enough of me, and that he'll deal with me shortly (whatever that meaneth). It's not that I'm a-feared of him, but I findeth fighting so uncool and moreover, blinking stupid. I knoweth poor Gol...sorry...Reuben's never going to win the Brain of Galilee prize, but beneath all that bluster and machismo, I'm sure there MUST be a nice guy trying to get out. Mustn't there?

Having said that, I'm not that thrilled at the prospect of having my teeth lodged halfway down mine own throat, or having my nose pointed in another direction. It's odd, but at the back of my mind I seem to remember a story of a fight betwixt a huge bully and someone like me in the scriptures.

9th February 10 AD

Slept little last night. I couldn't stop wondering when and where this confrontation wouldst occur or what Reuben planned to do unto me. I doubt whether he actually wants to kill me to actual death, but that doesn't seem much consolation. As for me, I certainly don't want to kill, maim or even make his nose bleed. Woe unto him that hurteth another in anger, I say.

At school today he was even eviler than before, however; threatening to show me up for the wimp he thinketh I am. Verily, he's decided that the great confrontation shalt come to pass after school tomorrow, on the piece of wasteland beside the lake. It sounds like a right throng is going to be there. My few mates (the Disciple Gang) and most of the girls, have pleaded with me to call it off, which I can't do, as it would not only admit that I was scared of him (which I am!) but spur him onward to bully others. I paced up and down for hours trying to think of a way of coming out of all this with self respect (and my teeth) but it all looketh a bit hopeleth. I reckon he'll make mincemeat out of me if I can't come up with an answer by sun-up.

10th February 10 AD

Woe is me, for today started out as probably the very worst in my life. Mrs Nathanson, my teacher, yelled continually at me for not paying attention, and all the big lads sniggered behind my back, really looking forward to the end of classes. The girls, bless'em, were all vying to tend my wounds upon my certain thrashing, but somehow that didn't seem to make me feel much better.

Upon the ringing of the final bell, I dragged myself down to the 'battleground', where a smallish multitude were waiting to see the fun (and the blood). Gol...sorry...Reuben was already there, stripped to the waist, and showing off his huge biceps to all the girls who looked well vexed at the prospect of my imminent demise.

As I walked towards him, the mini-multitude backed away, and he stood, huger than ever, cracking his knuckles with relish, at the prospect of knocking me forth into the midst of next week. In no time I was in front of him and, as he towered over me, I prayed to the Lord for some miracle to happen that would'st get me out of this awful mess.

And lo and behold, the first blow came, like a thunderbolt from above. I saw a shower of stars and fell upon the ground. After a couple of seconds, I opened my eyes gingerly, expecting my head to be not that close to my body but, strangely enough, felt no pain. I put my hand upon my face but it felt not remotely sore. I then stood up, as he walked away, fists held high, to the cheers of his bully-boy mates. And lo, when he turned round and saw me on my feet with a puzzled expression upon my face, his jaw dropped in amazement. Well vexed, he rushed at me and struck me again, even harder.

Again I went down like a felled tree, and lo, on opening my eyes, felt nothing. After about a score or so of these 'knockouts', the crowd was cheering me — yes me — every time I got up on my feet, and laughing at him as he held his now bloodied fist in agony (sorry about that Lord!).

Then, in desperation, he picked up what looked like a huge branch that lay by his feet and came at me as if to kill me. But, lo and behold, it suddenly wasn't a stick but a huge extremely cross serpent, which he held in his hand. Horror-struck he flung it to the ground and when it slithered after him, he ran as fast as he could and dived behind the nearest bush. But he must have kicked a flint and caused a spark, for it suddenly went up in flames and this burning bush, set his raiment alight. In pure terror he rushed to the lake and dived towards the water, but the water seemed to part and he landed flat on his face in the mire where he lay sobbing with his clothing still a-smouldering.

Verily, everyone went crazy, including all Reuben's former mates, and they held me upon high. I'd beaten the bully but God knows how; I didn't have to strike a single blow. Hallelujah!!

Jesus had been right about a similar situation occurring in the scriptures. In the Book of Samuel, there is a description of the terrible tiff between the original Goliath, the champion of the Philistines, and the now famous David from whence our hero's family was descended.

The Philistines, by the way, were a nasty nation who were always trying to get the Israelites into a war. Goliath was thirteen feet tall, covered from head to toe in heavy bronze armour, and even had a little guy to hold up his huge shield in front of him (see rotten jobs in biblical times). He walked out every day from the enemy lines and challenged the Israelites to send someone forward to fight him (on a winner-takes-all basis).

The only mug they could find was a young shepherd called David who, as luck would have it, happened to be delivering lunch to his soldier brothers. David, incidentally, had heard that the prize for killing this bolshy brute was not only the saving of his people, but a load of loot, King Saul's well-tasty daughter, and an exemption for his whole family from their service to the Israeli army.

King Saul thought the boy was off his rocker but realized that if nobody met the incredible hulk, the ensuing massacre would be over by tea-time (and so would his job). So, there being not much to lose (apart from some two-bit shepherd), he promptly strapped his own armour on David and put his own sword in the boy's hand. David threw off the tinwear (as he couldn't stand up in it) and asked for five smooth stones to use with his sling.

When Goliath saw David, he practically wet himself laughing and told the lad that he'd feed him to the birds and the beasts. The boy, rather cheekily, informed the giant that he'd not only strike him down, but cut his head off too. (Actually, it must be said that, if I were a betting man, my money would have been on the birds and beasts, as it now looked, one way or other, like they'd be in for a damned good supper that night.)

The huge Philistine moved in, but our David, quick as a flash, whipped out his first stone and slung it straight at the forehead of the giant. Goliath fell dead to the ground and David niftily

removed the poor stiff's head with his own sword. From then on it was all pretty plain sailing (or slaying).

When all the Philistines were dead, David went back to Saul, head in hand (Goliath's - not his!) and Saul was all over him like a cheap suit, ordering him to stay within the bosom of his family (and his daughter!) which was no bad deal, seeing as he was the king and dead rich.

And so, both stories had a happy ending although Jesus's of course was the best. Our hero didn't have to strike a single blow.

Jesus's First 'Miracle'

Jesus's dad had always been good with his hands, and it had seemed totally natural for our hero to suppose he would follow his old man into the carpentry business. Joseph could turn his hand to almost anything, whether it be furniture for the home, agricultural implements, toys for the village children or customized coffins (for ex-customers).

But Joseph reckoned he was more than just a craftsman. He liked to think of himself as a bit of an inventor, and was always either dreaming up new 'labour-saving' devices, or keeping his ear to the ground for new ideas. This used to drive his Mrs – Mary – doolally, as she was usually landed with the unenviable job of being chief tester, often with disastrous results.

There was the time, for instance, when Joseph proudly presented her with the world's first food mixer, with a wooden bowl at one end, a series of wheels, cogs, pulleys and ropes in the middle, and a foot treadle attached to the other. Many a time Jesus would come home from school to find his mother collapsed and sobbing by the kitchen table smothered from head to foot with various sticky concoctions.

Or there was the first fully automatic goat catcher and restrainer, for easy milking. This was basically a wooden beam with

rope attached, which could be swung out over the flock in the back yard and placed anywhere required. The rope would then be lowered over the targeted, unsuspecting beast, slipped round his neck and then yanked upwards, theoretically making it impossible for the goat to run away. This brilliant aid was abandoned after effectively executing three of the family's very best milkers.

Here's the bit in Jesus's diary where he reaches his fourteenth birthday

25th December 10 AD

Dear Diary

And it hath come to pass that it is the day of my birth. Fourteen years, thank the Lord, great stuff! I arose at cock-crow to find that my dear old dad hath been a-burning the midnight oil making me a present, and left it at the end of my mattress. Actually it's a bit of a drag having a carpenter for thy parent, as I only ever seem to get something he's knocked up himself. I know thou shouldn't look a gift camel in the mouth, but some of the stuff he's created in the past hath left me well puzzled. This one is no exception.

For some time now, the old man hath bent the ears of Mum and yours truly about some sailors he'd met down at the boat yard, who had bent HIS ear about this far distant northern land where they do something called winter sports. Lately, over the breaking of bread, the old man had been winking his eye knowingly at my mum as he regaled us with far-fetched yarns about these odd persons who, it wouldst appear, get their kicks sliding down steep hillsides.

Notwithstanding (and to cut a long parable short) when I finally parted the papyrus wrapping, I was surprised to find something about the measure of a small table or large tray, a cubit (the distance between the elbow and finger tip) and a bit long, with two sort of runners, that curled up at the ends and were nailed upon the bottom with nails. He'd told me that this was the sort of gizmo they useth for their 'sport'.

But behold, though I was a bit dubious to say the least, as soon as I'd had my brekky, I didst tear up to the top of the Mount of Olives, whereupon I mounted my new table, and sat and sat . . . and sat. Needleth to say nothing came to pass (apart from a few goats who clocked me as if I'd gone totally bonkers). I then had the

sneaking feeling that my father (which art in Nazareth), God bless him had, as usual, not listened to their words as closely as he might, and had left out some crucial part when building this weird contraption. Verily, I thought, upon deciding to give up, and just as Lot lisped, when the Lord turneth his Mrs into a pillar, 'It's the thalt that counts!'

And it came to pass, as I strolled down the hill I noticed, far yonder, a few of my mates down by the lake. As usual they were tearing up and down in the water, diving forth from the rocks and, as was their habit, making complete prats of themselves trying to impress the village girls, who laboured with the family wash.

And then it happened that I had one of my visions. Like the Dead Sea, of Scrolls fame, our lake was saltier than a sailor's beard and practically anything would float like a cork. Lo, out of sight of my brethren (so as not to make a prat of myself), I launched my table upon the shallows and practised balancing.

After a while, and when I'd got the hang of it, a stiff breeze came to pass which pushed me, quite smartly, past the small throng that were upon the bank. As the Bible sayeth, It's an ill wind that bloweth nobody any good. When I smited the bank, further up the lake, all the girls rushed up and fell upon me, totally gobsmacked and much more to the point, quite adoring. What's the big deal? I asked myself. Then Rebecca, by far the fairest one (so I'd been told), asked how I didst manage to walk upon the water. I tried to explain, but when I turned about, my table had floated away and was not to be seen. Ah well, I thought, it was a fab stunt, but will it ever come in useful again?*

* In many countries, Jesus is officially credited with the invention of the surfboard.

Jesus obviously became better and better at water-walking, and some say he even learned to do it without his dad's present. In Mark, Chapter 6, Verse 48, when he missed the boat that was carrying his merry men (the disciples) over to Capernaam, it says:

> And he saw them toiling in rowing; for the wind was contrary unto them: and about the fourth watch of the night he cometh unto them, walking on the water, and would have passed them by.

Jesus Goes Fishing

Jesus had just come back from a short fishing trip on the sea of Galilee with his dad Joseph. Technology wise, fishing hadn't moved far from ancient times, and consisted mostly of chucking a net in the water and hoping the dumb critters would swim into it. Fishing lines were sometimes used, but they were a touch hit or miss.

Just before their jaunt, however, Jesus's father had been speaking to some traveller who'd been over on the other side of the world where he'd seen someone using a wonderful device for catching fish. Instead of just throwing a line into the sea with a hook on the end, he'd seen some guy with a long pole, to which was attached the line.

The long line had a hook at one end and was attached to a spindle at the other which in turn was attached to the stick. By jerking the stick (called casting), the baited hook could be sent a long, long way from the bank. When a fish took the bait, the operator simply pulled hard and reeled in the line with the fish on the end. This device, to the ears of Joseph and Jesus, was about as exciting as the invention of the ball to cricket fans. They couldn't wait to get down to the workshop and knock up a couple of rods (as they were called) and reels.

16th February 11 AD

Dear Diary

I've just got to bed after a long, hard day. Holy Moses, thank heavens it's over. Verily, I thought tonight the old man might finally flip his poor old lid.

It all started well before cock-crow this morning. We staggered downstairs and broke our fast quite smartish. We had to creep around, as Dad always gets into heavy bother with her-that-must-be-obeyed, if and whenever he's caught sneaking off (usually with my good self), for a day's sport.

The poor old geezer was already in her bad books, as last night Mum had found this rotting ram's head, which had stunk the house out for a couple of days. She'd wondered whether he'd joined some strange new sect or other, and was either worshipping it, or using the disgusting object as a kind of peace offering or sacrifice. Dad couldn't tell her that he'd simply left it hanging about to collect maggots for bait, for truly it wouldst have given the game away. The only thing that might save his bacon (not that we ever have any), would be to bring home enough good fish to eat now and to salt for later. Those old silver swimmers had always been the old lady's absolute favourite.

Anyway, it came to pass that, as the sun was rising in the east, we sloped out of the house and shoved all our poles, bait, sandwiches,* water bottles and huge nets (to keep the fish in) upon Nebuchadnezza, our ancient donkey.

It was a couple of hours hot, hard slog from Nazareth to the banks of the lake (which was more like a smallish sea) but when we finally arrived, we were happy to see a multitude of silvery fish leaping out of, and upon, the water, confident in the knowledge that if we got anywhere near them they could simply make themselves scarce.

'I think we're in here, Jesus,' said Dad, as he rigged up his new prize possession.

He swiftly cast his maggot way out amongst the fishy throng. 'The old lady'll never give us a hard time if we turn up with a sackful of these boys,' he exclaimed, licking his lips.

I'm rather ashamed to say, oh Lord, that I hadn't nearly so much faith in our fishing skills. My dad was well renowned for his over confidence and blind trust in providence. I remembereth, like yesterday, the time he broke the habit of a lifetime and had a bet

* Not invented yet.

20

at the local camel races. A vision had come to him, he claimed, in which a young filly called Carpenter's Lass romped home in the three o'clock. He had practically blown a week's money, so was less than delighted when the stupid beast trailed in last with its tail betwixt its legs. If Dad had had a tail, there's no doubt that it would have been well betwixt his legs when he eventually trailed home. Mum was sore vexed to say the very least.

'Holy Moses, if you ever do anything like that again,' she'd yelled, 'I'll stop your allowance, and EVERYTHING else.'

I'm not quite sure what she meant by everything else but, verily, it seemed to have a far greater effect than the prospect of losing his pocket money.

Meanwhile, back at the lakeside, things were coming to a pretty slowish pass. Time after time, for hours on end, we reeled in our lines to find the hook as clean as a whistle. Verily, it must have looked as if we'd invented a new, longwinded, and dead complicated, way to feed fishes.

The only thing that either Dad or I had managed to pull out was an old sandal that had obviously been on the bottom (after the foot) for ages. Lo, when I suggested that I'd try to catch the other one for him, he seemed not to get the joke and stalked up the lake in a foul temper.

All day we toiled under the hot sun with nere a bite. Verily, I swore I saw jolly grins on the faces of the foolhardy fishes that still leapt upon the water. Dad was going crazy by now; rushing up and down, casting his maggots hither and thither, so fast that the poor things would hardly have had time to get their ever-open gobs round'em.

Forsooth, I thought, what wouldst the old lady say if we went home empty-handed? Verily, it did not bear thinking about. I prayed long and hard to the Lord for inspiration and help.

Suddenly, I had an idea. What if I was to get our huge but fine-meshed net, and somehow hold it over where the fishes jumpeth from the water? They might all jump in. For good measure, I filled the net with the rest of the maggots. I waited till Dad was looking the other way and attached the net, full of its squirmy bait, to the end of my pole. Then, carefully, I pushed it out over the water.

Lo and behold, as if by some sort of miracle, the hitherto dead cocky fish started plopping into the net like no tomorrow. After about fifteen minutes, I couldst hardly hold their weight, so called Dad over to help. At first he chided me that I cheated, but lo, when he realized the consequences of turning up, back at the ranch, fatigued and fishless, he positively blanched and grabbed hold of the straining pole alongside me.

And it came to pass, that ere long, the net was a wriggling, seething mass of beautiful, plump, silver and pink fishes and, as we loaded our sacks, he thanked me rather sheepishly for my idea. When I told him that it had been a sort of vision, he looked at me in a

strange kind of way and fell upon his knees and praised the Lord (I do wish he'd stop doing that!). Not only would there be something wonderful for our table tonight, but when salted, the rest of the fishes would give us sustenance for months to come.

We trudged home with happy hearts, both looking forward to the welcome (and Brownie points) that our haul wouldst gain us. Imagine our surprise when, on our return, we found, upon the kitchen table, a note which said:

Where in heaven's name have you two been all day? Didn't you remember I had to go to the doctor's again. Fat lot you both care! Anyway, he says I've got an allergy and thinks it might be to the eating of fish. I've been told I must eat no more. I knoweth not what you two have been up to, or what time you'll be coming back, so I've just popped round to Mrs Isaacson's up the road. I'll deal with you two reprobates upon my return.
    Be warned,
    Mother

17th February 11 AD

Just as a sort of a postcript to yesterday's event. Dad was given a right ear-bashing by the old lady upon her return last night. She was less than impressed by our fishy haul, indeed it seemed to add insult to injury. When she'd finally gone up to bed, my poor old man sat up with me discussing why the fishing poles hadn't worked. We came to no good conclusions, so this morning he went forth to the village and eventually cameth upon the bloke that had told him all about it.

The guy asked him to describe precisely what we had done and then cracked up laughing. Of course we caught nought, he said, because we'd left out an essential part of the kit. He then described to us the principle of the FLOAT, that was supposed to be attached upon the line, fairly close to the baited hook. Lo, it would bob on the surface, and wouldst only go under when the bait was interfered with by a fish. When the fisherman saw the float bobbing, he had to yank hard, knowing there's something there. Otherwise, he said, he'd have no idea when the stupid fish were actually nibbling and could be sitting upon the bank for days. He swore blind that he'd told Dad about it, but Dad, I'm afraid, swore even blinder, that he hadn't.

Jesus and his dad went rather easy on the fishing after this, but later in his life our hero spent quite a bit of time on boats, as practically all his disciples were in the fish business. In Luke, Chapter 5, it describes a day when he was standing by the Lake of Gennesaret. He'd noticed a couple of boats pulled up by the shore and nearby, his old mate Pete the fisherman, mending his nets looking well fed up. When he told Jesus that he'd been up half the night but had caught nothing more than a chill, Jesus told him to get back in the boat, sail into deeper water and have another go. Pete looked at him as if he was a fishy-short-of-a-picnic, but Jesus bet him it would work.

And when they had done this, they enclosed a great multitude of fishes; and their net broke. And they beckoned unto their partners, which were in another ship, that they should come and help them. And they came and filled both the ships, so that they began to sink.

Luckily they got the boats back to the shore, or it could have been yet another one of Jesus's 'good turns' that backfired.

Jesus Gets Conned

One day a messenger came from Jesus's Great Uncle Eli to say that he needed extra hands moving part of his huge herd. As Joseph wasn't that busy in the carpentry shop, he sent his son up to the land of the Gadarenes, on the other side of the lake, to help.

23rd May 11 AD

Dear Diary
  What a day!
  I must confess, as I went on my way out of Nazareth towards the valley that is the home of mine uncle, I was just a little confused. Joseph my father had told me that Uncle Eli was a breeder of swine, but what was he doing breeding swine? I had always been told that pigs were unclean, on account of the cloven hooves and the old non-chewing of cud bit (see page 116), so what possible use could he have for them? Pigs are all very well, but they're no good for milk and

they're no good for wool; thou canst not ride 'em and I've yet to see one pulling a cart. I knew thou couldst make wallets out of their

skin, or even shaving brushes from the bristles, but with a herd as large as Eli's, he could supply the whole of Israel with wallets twice over, and nobody shaves anyway (except the girls my mum inviteth round!). Come to that, what would he do with all the bits that were left? Personally, I've always found porkers rather stupid and just plain smelly.

25th May 11 AD

I pondered this for mile after mile all yesterday, and verily today – until I came upon Uncle Eli's place. I'd only set mine eyes upon his home once before, years ago, and at that time it had been a right shambles; so I was surprised to see the size of his new house and estate, which impressed me greatly to say the least.

Lo, beyond the palm trees that surroundeth the mansion, I could see a Roman style swimming pool, with an ornamental fountain, and a couple of flash carriages in the four carriage garage. A couple of yummy hand maidens flitted hither and thither wearing nothing but the tiniest of togas (and the largest of smiles). Verily, my old uncle wasn't now short of a shekel or two and, as I could see no sign of any other beasts or money-making enterprise, I could only putteth it down to pig breeding. All very mysterious.

Uncle Eli leant upon the beautiful wrought iron front gate, adorned by his new family crest (a shield held up by two pigs rampant), and seemed genuinely pleased to see me. So, after expressing felicitations from my parents, I launched straight into questions to satisfy my puzzlement.

'Uncle Eli,' I asked politely, 'why doest thou keep so many swine? Surely they are unclean and we Jews are forbidden to eat them?'

Eli looked about him nervously and replied, 'Ah yes, Jesus, well – um it's simple. I keepeth them as – er – pets, yes that's it – pets. I've always had a real soft spot for piggies.'

'But Uncle, there must be thousands of them. Why keepest thou so many?' I enquired innocently.

'A very good question, my boy,' he replied, seeming to search for an answer. 'I – er – often asketh myself the same question. You must understand, I didn't always have so many. I started with two but, over the years, you know how beasts are, they just seem to have multiplied into a multitude. Now, can we get on with the job in hand?'

'But surely they must costeth a fortune to feed?' I persisted, sensing that he wanted to change the subject. 'How canst thou possibly afford to keep them all? Won't the herd grow and grow until you can afford them no longer?'

'Ah, you may well ask,' he said in a flustered manner. 'Verily, it's a real nightmare trying to make enough money to feed them all.' I glanced over his shoulder, and looked upon his palatial house, as he continued, 'But look here, it really is MY problem, so there be no point worrying thy young head about it.'

I was no less confused. How was my uncle, who appeareth not to do anything save tend his pigs all day, living in considerable style while under such a financial burden?

Uncle Eli now looked rather angry, so I thought it wise not to carry on the interrogation.

That afternoon I helped his men split a couple of hundred of the larger porkers from the herd of thousands he appeared to own, and drive them about about six miles up the road to the borders of his land. And lo, uncle was met by a rather shady, decidedly Roman-looking, character with a fleet of specially fitted out carts, suspiciously resembling converted chariots, which they proceeded to load the swine upon. When twas done, the guy appeared to count out a large amount of golden coins which glinted in the sun as they dropped into a bag (pigskin no doubt), which jingled merrily as Uncle Eli walked back towards me. I might be daft, but it looked very much as if he'd SOLDETH those pigs, which seemed rather an odd thing to do with thy pets.

Yes indeed, I might be daft; but I'm not stupid. Suddenly it dawned upon me that my wicked uncle was running an illegal business — pig-running! Selling bootleg pork to be devoured in the fleshpots (literally) of the land by people of no faith. Worse still, he'd used me, yes, me-that-is-without-sin, to help shift the stock for his filthy trade.

'How couldst thou do this to me, uncle?' I cried. 'I've never done anything dishonest in my life and it now appeareth that I've aided and abetted you in your unholy activities. Knowest thou not that it's against Moses's laws to eat pork? It is a grievous sin that you commit!'

'Well, I'm sorry you see it that way, young Jesus, but the way I looketh upon it, I'm simply supplying demand. If I didn't do it, someone else would.'

This, of course, is the excuse that every villain in the history of villainy hath given, and I would hear none of it.

'Thou must repent your ways, Unc, and abide by the word of God thy father. Otherwise, when thou finally poppeth thine clogs, thou wilt go down to the fiery furnace.'

Uncle Eli had obviously had enough of my timely advice and, nearly bursting a blood vessel, yelled forth.

'Look, you self-righteous little creep! Why doesn't thou get off my back and pi . . .ig off! I've had just about enough of thy smart-arsed comments. Go back to fairy land from whence thou came, and leave me to run my business in peace.'

With that, he tossed me a couple of coins for the work I'd done, and stalked off.

'Beware the wages of sin,' I shouted after him, leaving the coins in the dust. He then turned and gave unto me a curious sign that I recognized not.

HE THINKS I CAN'T COUNT!

*Had a bit of a weird day today. Attended school, but my teacher,
Mrs Jacobson, kept yelling at me for not paying attention. I haven't
been able take mine mind off Uncle Eli and his dodgy pig business
for days. I knewest that I should really go next door to the
synagogue and report him to the rabbis, but lo, it really isn't in my
nature to grasseth anyone up. I suppose if those occupying Roman
soldiers desire to eat filthy pigs, then it's their concern, but mine is
Uncle Eli's endangered soul.*

But Jesus never forgot his uncle's bad ways and much later in
life (when in the good works biz), he heard that a poor (rich)
man, on the other side of the lake, had in fact gone totally round
the bend having become more than obsessed with a herd of pigs
(the swine). He'd followed them wherever they went and now
lived, barking mad, among the tombs that were built into the
hillside near where they grazed (or whatever pigs do). I suppose
Jesus put two and two together and surmised it might be his
ancient uncle.

As he'd spent this last fifteen years worrying about the way-
ward Eli, he decided to see if he could help. In Luke, Chapter 8,
it describes the goings on when Jesus finally caught up with an
old mad man, having sailed across the lake to the land of the
Gadarenes. After asking around, he'd heard that this weirdo,
who'd broken free from the chains that held him, had torn off
all his clothes, and was living close by. Jesus eventually met him
and, although he couldn't be sure that it was his old uncle,
realized the old guy was barking mad and needed help.

He *(Uncle Eli)* cried with a loud voice, and said:
'What have I to do with Thee Jesus, Thou Son of the most High
God. I adjure *(beg)* Thee by God, that Thou torment me not.' *(He
obviously hadn't forgotten the tongue-lashing he'd got the last time.)*
Then He *(Jesus)* said unto him 'Come out of the man, thou
unclean spirit.' And then He asked him, 'What is thy name?'
(Obviously just testing.) And he *(Eli)* answered saying 'My name is
'Legion'; for we are many.' *(obviously bonkers.)*
And he *(Eli)* besought Him *(Jesus)* much that He would not send
him away out of the country.
Now there was nye unto the hillside a great herd of swine feeding.
And all the devils *(living in our Eli)* besought Him *(Jesus)* saying:

29

'Send us into the swine, that we may enter into them.'

And forthwith Jesus gave them permission. And the unclean spirits went out, and entered into the swine: and the herd *(now bonkers themselves)* ran violently down a steep place and into the sea *(and there were about two thousand)* and were choked in the sea *(ever seen a pig swim?)*.

Now this must have seemed a bit of a result to Jesus. Not only had he made the old guy better, but he'd got rid of some two thousand filthy porkers. The trouble was, all the people of the Gadarene district, who'd obviously been living well on the land (and pigs), were really hacked off at the loss of their income, and told Jesus, in so many words, to...'go away'. Jesus shrugged amiably, then got back in his boat and sailed back to the other side of the lake. Job done! Nice one Jesus!

Jesus and the Haircut

It was the fashion at Jesus's school for all the lads to wear their hair long. Jesus was no exception, thinking like the others, that it was real cool. But his mother, Mary, was always going on about it, preferring him to look like a good, orthodox Jewish boy, with his hair cut short except for the bits by the ears which were traditionally grown in long straggly ringlets. Although Jesus was never that interested in girls, he certainly didn't want to look untrendy (and, more to the point, had sticky-out ears). Every day his mother would bring the subject up.

BAD BIBLICAL BOY   GOOD BIBLICAL BOY

17th June 12 AD

Dear Diary
Lo, I was just about to go to school this very morning when Mum cornered me yet again and went on about my appearance.
'I thought thou were going to let me cut thy hair, it's a total disgrace. Heaven knows what the neighbours thinkest,' she scolded, tugging upon the locks that hung over my raiment.

31

'Oh, please don't go on so, Mum!' I replied dejectedly. 'All the boys wear it like this these days.'

'What boys? I don't give a fig about all the others,' she cried. 'If their mothers mindeth not their lads looking like maidens then verily, that will be their business, but as long as you're under our roof, you'll abide by the rules of this house. Girls hath long hair, boys hath short. That's simply the way it is and always will be.'

With that, she stalked across the room, clicking her tongue in mock disgust.

'But why mother?' I pleaded. 'Long hair makest me not a bad person nor preventeth me from doing my lessons. Why do I have to conform to what you and Dad want?'

'Because, young Jesus m'lad, we art thy parents and knowest best.' She sat down at the table and, in her grandest theatrical manner, put her head in her hands and sighed. 'Oh Lord, who wouldst have children? They will be the very death of me. Verily, when I was a girl, children respected their parents and tried to do what pleased them. What hast I done to deserve such trials?'

'Look Mum,' I cried, trying to keep my cool. 'It's not as if I robbeth folk, or torture beasts or beat up old people. All I want is to be able to do my own thing.'

'I'll give you your own thing, thou lippy lad! Now enough of all this argumenting – go forth and get thy stupid hair CUT!'

18th June 12 AD

And it came to pass, after school today, I nipped out the back to see the rabbis and ask them what they thought. Luckily, being men of God, they all had long, white hair, so were somewhat disposed to try and help me out. First they read from Moses's rules to the Israelites in Leviticus, Chapter 20: **'Ye shall not round the corners of your heads; neither shalt thou mar the corners of thy beard.'**

Now I don't know about thou, but if having a severe haircut isn't rounding your head, I knoweth not what is; but it seemed not that conclusive. Verily, I must find another biblical angle to tackle Mum with.

The old men pondered for hours upon the ancient texts to no avail, until one of them suggested that I could always try the old Samson angle, whereupon all the others chortled wisely. I asked what he meant, so he related the old story from the Book of Judges as best he remembered it.

Once upon a long, long time ago, there was a bunch of right yobbos called Philistines who resided along the southern coast of Palestine and, almost daily, threatened to do over the Israelites. One of these Israelites called Manoah had been praying to God, asking firstly, to bring forth a fab new leader who'd be gutsy enough to stand up to the feisty Philistines, and secondly, if it wasn't too much trouble, to bring them a son as, for some reason, Mrs Manoah couldn't have 'em.

One day, there was a knock upon the back door and, lo, it was an Angel of God, (angels seldom use the front...far too public!) who,

VERY NICE, BUT WHAT'S THE CATCH?

— EARLY PET

after exchanging the usual pleasantries, said they would have a boy, but upon condition that they must bring him up ever so carefully, as he was actually destined to be the guy to save Israel. From the day of his birth, the angel said, the lad must dedicate himself to God and must never, repeat never, cut his hair (at this point my interest began to be aroused).

Manoah was dead grateful and offered the young angel a burnt goat as a present, or sacrifice, before leaving (certainly one up on a cup of mint tea and a rock cake). The angel thanked him, but as soon as the poor goat was afire he jumped in the flames and used the rising smoke to take him up to heaven again (as angels do).

Now I must admit I found this tale a touch on the whacky side, but lo, it seemed to be developing along the right lines, so I asked the

33

old man to carry on.

The following day, he continued, Mrs Manoah felt a little strange and realized she was up the duff — of should I say — with child.
And it came to pass, in due course, the nipper came forth, and they called the little mite Samson. Little, but certainly not feeble. Even when tiny he was a real brute — a kind of junior-league Goliath (see p. 12).

The story moved straightway to when Samson was a young man with long lustrous hair (at last!) and a great bod. Lo, he was so strong that on one occasion, when growled at by a powerful young lion (as powerful young lions are wont to do) he, being no big name in animal conservation, tore it to pieces with his bare hands.

But don't go thinking that it was all plain sailing for his parents either, as it seemed that the only bit of his anatomy he hadn't

I SAY, YOU REALLY OUGHT TO THINK ABOUT ORAL HYGIENE

TIMNAH

developed was betwixt his ears. This he proved by getting engaged to a young Philistine lass.*

As the wedding approached, our daft bridegroom-to-be developed a somewhat annoying habit of rushing forth every five minutes to slay various numbers of her people. When her dad, fairly understandably, called off the wedding, Samson lost his rag and went on another jolly away-slay and just, to make those Phillies even

* A bit like Adolph Hitler's son (if he'd had one) falling in love with a nice Jewish girl.

more mad, rounded up three hundred jackals, tied their tails together, attached fiery torches to these knotted tails and then sent them scampering (which YOU jolly well would, if your tail was on fire) into enemy olive groves, grain fields and vineyards.

The Philistines retaliated by rushing round to Samson's sort-of-ex wife and father-in-law's gaff promptly torching them to death (so the dame got it in the end anyway). When they caught up with Samson, he promptly turned round and slew a thousand of them with a donkey's jawbone (probably with the donkey attached). Samson then went from bad to worse, sleeping with harlots and wrecking Philistine cities, single-handed, willy-nilly. Eventually, however, he happened upon another dead gorgeous Philistine girl named Delilah, and fell in love once more. But the lords of the Philistines heard of this development and, spying a great opportunity, offered her 1100 pieces of silver (a tidy sum) if she could find out the secret of his immense strength.

When Delilah pleaded with him to tell his secret, he promptly asked her to tie him up upon the bed (how strange!) with seven new bowstrings claiming that, in that state, he'd be no stronger than anyone else. (a likely story.)

Little didst he know the brazen hussy had organized a load of the filthy Philistines to be within the next room a-listening.

When she had him nicely trussed up like an oven-ready turkey, she suddenly yelled 'The Philistines cometh! The Philistines cometh!', whereupon they all tumbled in. Naughty old Samson simply shrugged, broke free from his bondage, and slew the lot.

But he didn't even smell a rat (showing his stupidity yet again), so when Delilah accused him of making a fool of her by telling her a large porky, he told her to weave his hair into a loom and fasten it with a peg (funny bloke) which, he promised wouldst certainly subdue his strength. This she promptly did.

No sooner was he secured than she yelled once again 'The Philistines cometh! The Philistines cometh!' and another bunch flew in through the door. But, yet again, wily old Samson broke free and slew that lot as well. But he still didn't connect Delilah with this apparently endless stream of ruffians bursting into her bedroom at the drop of a hat (or peg).

Day after day she nagged him about the secret of his strength and in the end it came to pass, for a quiet life, he gave in and told her that his hair had never been cut and that, if ever it was, he'd succumb to instant wimpdom.

She straightway sent for a new lot of Philistine heavies

(presumably hairdressers) and told them to cut off his hair while
he was a-sleeping. This time when she yelled 'The Philistines
cometh' he was powerless to do anything about it.

The Philistines were well happy (and Delilah well rich!), and promptly
blinded short-back-and-sided Samson and threw him into a filthy
dungeon.

Ages later, the Philistine leaders decided to go and get Samson
out as entertainment for one of their big bashes. But lo, they
hadn't been monitoring his coiffure (let alone cutting it).
Unbeknownst to them, he'd got most of his hair (and strength) back.

So when they chained him between two huge pillars and used him
cruelly (mass tickling – I expect), and were singing and dancing and
generally taking the mickey, Samson huffed and puffed and cracketh
the mighty pillars, bringing down the roof and killing all the Philistine
leaders, which was good news. The bad news (for Samson) was that
he was killed too.

19th June 12 AD

All through last night I wondered how I could use the Samson story
to outwit my mum – hairwise. Eventually I evolved a foolproof plan
and, after school, I copied out a shortened version of the tale of
Samson and Delilah and left it, casually, on my mattress upstairs.

When Mum and I were alone, I spake unto her.

'Mother, I've been a-thinking. I've been reading the laws of Moses again and have come to the bit where it says it's wrong to defy thy parents. So I've decided that if it will make you happy, I'll let you, but only you, trim my hair.'

She looked at me dead suspiciously but in the end smiled.

'There's a good lad, Jesus. I knew thou wouldst come round in the end. I'll go sharpen the haircutting knife.'

I sat down upon the chair and waited for the fun to begin. As soon as she'd made the first tentative snip, I put my hand to my head and made as if to swoon. In true dramatic style, I slumped forward in the chair and then slid slowly to the floor.

'Jesus, Jesus,' she cried. 'My son, what in God's name is the matter with you? Speak to your mother already. Canst thou hear me?'

'Yes, ma,' I replied, barely audibly. 'I just suddenly feel terribly, terribly weak. Fret not, I'm sure I'll be all right in a mo.'

20th June 12 AD

All through yesterday, I lay around the house, hardly moving. Mother sent forth for the apothecary, who after a full examination, looked totally puzzled.

'Sorry, M'am,' he proclaimed. 'I can find absolutely nothing wrong with your lad. I'm afraid there's nothing I canst do. That'll be ten shekels for the call out, however.'

Mother continued a-pacing up and down looking distraught (not helped by the ten shekels call-out fee). But I was becoming nervous as I really hadn't planned to cause her so much distress. Suddenly Joseph rushed down the stairs, clutching the papyrus that had been left upon my bed. The plan was working.

'Quick Mary, cop a load of this,' he yelled, highly agitated.

Mum snatched it and read the story as fast as she couldst, glancing at me every few seconds. She then came over, bent down and stroked my hair gently.

'Oh Jesus, darling boy, I'm so sorry,' she whispered. 'I should never have cut your hair. I sometimes forget thou art a very, very special person (what did she mean by that?) and we must treat you as such. Obviously thou hast the same problem as Samson. I promise I will never touch your hair again.'

After a week or so, Jesus's strength 'returned' and he went back to school. Imagine his surprise when he entered the classroom and saw all his male chums with short back-and-sides. When he asked what had come to pass, it turned out that, while he was away, a groovy young travelling minstrel had hit the village and all the girls had gone crazy over him. The young singer, as you might have guessed, was a real babe, with short hair and ringlets running down either side of his ears. The lads had all rushed home and got their mums to cut theirs accordingly so as to be in the fashion (and get their girls back).

Jesus, as you might imagine, was well and truly stymied.

Jesus and the Prodigal Brother

Although it is generally understood that Jesus's mum Mary was and always remained – how should I put it – 'untouched by human hand', there seems to be some confusion as to whether Jesus had any brothers or sisters. Most of the controversy stems from one short, and easily passed over, passage in the New Testament. In the Mark Chapter 6, when Jesus first started teaching in the synagogue, a group of punters, astonished at his biblical knowledge and wisdom asked 'Is not this the carpenter, the son of Mary, the brother of James and Joses and Judas, and Simon? And are not his sisters here with us?'

Brother Jim (short for James) crops up many times and in many versions of the Bible, and it is about him that Jesus relates the next story.

Jim Davidson* had always wondered about all the mystery and silence surrounding his older (by one year) brother's whacky arrival; and resented the way his parents always treated him as if he was something rather special.

He couldn't have been more different to Jesus, being a right comedian: cheeky, disobedient, distrustful, dishonest and a total trial to his poor parents. On his birthday, he demanded his share of the family inheritance (a bit premature methinks), which even in those days, was a tidy sum.

NOT INVENTED YET

* Jesus's family were almost certainly Davidsons, as they were directly descended from King David.

The day after he got the loot, he upped and left the household, leaving his elder brother Jesus worried and upset.

7th July 12 AD

Dear Diary

Verily, there hasn't been as much fuss come to pass in our household since Jim was caught canoodling with the Rabbi's granddaughter at the back of the donkey shed. It now looketh like he's done it again. When we arose from our slumbers this morning, Jim's mattress was untouched, save for a note which read as follows.

Deer Mum + dad.
Sory if this cums as
a bit of a shok, but
it surys you rite. I
just can't stand it
here no more, so I've
gon To seke my
fourTune in The
wide wurld — Jim

There was much gnashing of teeth and tearing of hair, and Mother had one of her famous 'bad turns'.

'What will become of that ungrateful boy,' she cried. 'Have I not always been a wonderful mother? Didn't we always give him a fine home? Hasn't he been brought up a good Jewish boy? Oh Lordie, that he should do this to me already! What will the neighbours say? Oh woe is me, woe is me!'

Dad was more calm and replied, 'Don't vex yourself so, Mother, the ungrateful little tyke disgraceth us all. He's always been a problem, that one. We're better off without him. Good riddance I say!'

Jesus was more forgiving and prayed every night for his brother's safe return to the bosom of his family. But days turned into weeks, and weeks into months, without a single word from the missing boy. Then, one day, our hero was down in the village, picking up some supplies for his dad, when a local commercial traveller told him that he'd seen his brother Jim in Tyre, a large seaport, way up north on the coast. Apparently, he'd blown most of his inheritance on wine, women (well, girls!) and song, in that order, and was in a sorrowful state. Jesus begged the man not to tell his parents and came home in a sad and thoughtful mood.

1st November 12 AD

Dear Diary

There's nothing for it. Lo, I've been awake all night and there is only one solution. I prayed unto my Lord and he reckoneth that I must go forth to find my errant brother and rescue him from his evil ways. I will depart before cock-crow tomorrow before my parents (or the cock) stir. I only hope they will realize that this is the only thing I can do.

2nd November 12 AD

Luckily Dad had bought a spare donkey only a month earlier, just in case the old one were to break down. But I loathe young Jezebel (as she's fittingly labelled), even against my better nature, as she will never do remotely what she is told. Even the strapping of my supplies upon her back was like trying to balance an apple upon a serpent — every time I thought I had them fixed, she'd flex her

muscles and scatter the whole lot upon the ground. It was enough to make even me swear beneath my breath (if only I knew the right words!).

Eventually, however, the dopey donkey trotted out of the lean-to and off in completely the wrong direction whilst braying at the top of her stupid voice, as if she tryeth to prove conclusively that the mind of a donkey is lodged somewhere up its backside.

Notwithstanding, and despite the bad start, the going became fairly easy when we hit the flat plains north of Nazareth (even if it was hot enough at midday to barbecue a tortoise) and we must have covered some 2000 cubits by nightfall. Having camped beside a little stream, Jezebel proceeded to eat the map which I had carefully drawn last night, and verily, I am seriously considering whether she might be more use to me if I ate HER, though I know her parting gift to me would be severe gut-ache (plus the Lord's severe displeasure – cloven hoof, cud chewing etc, see page 116). But worse than all that, I have just found the note within my pocket that I was supposed to leave for Mum and Dad, so they probably thinketh that I've gone the same way as Jim (which isn't far from the truth when thou thinkest on it).

4th November 12 AD

We're now over halfway, and Jezebel and I have become sworn enemies. I really know now why the donkey is also known as an ass. This silly ass has the memory of a goldfish (if that's not being fishist) as it seems that the part of its brain that keepeth the stupid beast going in one direction hath a five second time loop. If I wasn't there to lead her, she would be simply walking round in circles, continually surprised at the newness of what she's recently encountered.

As the sun was setting, we met a camel train upon the new Roman road on its way south. Although the camels were some of the most magnificent I had ever clapped mine eyes upon, the merchant in charge was verily a different matter. His personal hygiene left so much to be desired that even Jezebel (who even fleas or flies refuse to settle upon) resisted the morsels he offered from his pocket. He told us, however, that he had met someone that fitteth my brother's description, and that this person had been the talk of Tyre, as he had been spending money as if twas water. Every unvirtuous girl had been out with him, every gambler had fleeced him, every bar owner had chucked him out and he had been reduced to offering bits of his body (unsuccessfully) for medical research to make ends meet.

I jabbed Jezebel in the rump, and we quickly proceeded on our way. I realized that if we were to save Jim from himself, time was of the essence. On the morrow, we must move faster than ever to reach our destination.

7th November 12 AD

Verily, Jezebel's rump is as tender as a pummelled steak, due to the extra 'encouragement' that I had given it with my trusty cane. Consequently, we made much better progress, and by sundown we were coming upon the outskirts of the great city of Tyre. My female companion, I must add, was now in a worse mood than my mother and father had been when we left.

Never have I seen so many people in my life. Ragged children and limbless beggars scuttled along beside us; thieves and pickpockets viewed us hungrily from dark alleyways; women of loose morals winked and beckoned us invitingly (well, probably just me!); and every single person seemed hell-bent on getting in our way. We, therefore, made dead slow progress through the midst of the throng. We passed evil-looking street traders who begged us to stop, and threatened each other with curses that would curdle milk; cafes and cook-houses that roasted bits of animals (presumably) whose origin I could not even venture to guess at; soothsayers and apothecaries who beseeched punters to enter their filthy surgeries and be conned rotten; ancient men, stoned out of their boxes, who sucketh noisily on filthy hubble-bubble pipes; and all this bound together with the fetid stench of the open sewers that glistened brownly at the side of the street.

We are now, at the time of writing, in a small inn that looketh and stinketh as if it's recently been used as a public loo. I say we, because I've had to bring the awful Jezebel into my room and tie her leg to my leg for fear of her being nicked (as if anyone would be that demented). Tomorrow, however, we shall set out to try to find my brother.

8th November 12 AD

Most of the morning was spent walking hither and thither amongst the throng, asking all and sundry if they'd clapped eyes on my

feckless brother. Lo, just as I was about to give up, an old, toothless hag, came from within the shadows and told me that she thought she'd seen him toiling at the port, gathering camel and donkey droppings as fertilizer for the local farmers. I jabbed Jezebel, forthwith, and headed through the multitude until we came upon the dockside. After only ten minutes, I spied a familiar figure. Familiar, but clothed in rags and looking, moreover, like something the cat dragged in.

'Jim,' I cried, 'is that really you? What doeth thou here?'

'Oh no, not you, Jesus! If life isn't bad enough without having to cope with a lecture from Mr Goody-Two-Sandals. Anyway, you pious prat, what does it look like I'm doing – gathering daffodils? Why don't you f . . .requent somewhere else!'

'But what hath happened to all thy money?' I pleaded. 'What hath reduced thou to doing this?'

He looked upon me with the purest loathing. 'Oh, I've just got this thing about working with animals, and lo, this is the nearest I can get,' he snarled sarcastically.

'I've come forth to bring you home.' I cried. 'You can't carry on like this.'

'Mmm, brilliant idea,' he yelled back, shovelling shi – sorry – digging dung furiously. 'I'd rather face a good stoning than the braying tongues of those stupid old wrinklies back home. Thank thou Jesus, but no thank thou. Now get lost!'

I went to hug him but, verily, met a wall of odour that not only stopped me dead, but brought Jezebel to her knees. I then beseeched him for hours, telling him that, although our parents might be a bit sticky to begin with, they'd come round in the end. Either way, I said, he would soon kill himself, if he didn't sort himself out.

Gradually, and grudgingly, he calmed down, and after I'd managed to clean him up, and purchase him some fresh clothes, we set off upon the long, long road back to Nazareth.

13th November 12 AD

Oh Lord, why do I try to be a do-gooder?

When it came to pass that we eventually got home, the reaction was far from what I expected, as mother and father acted most peculiarly – even for them. As soon as they saw us they fell upon their knees and thanked the Lord. But it turned out to be only for MY safe return – not Jim's. Mother wepteth buckets whilst Dad rushed out the back and promptly topped a calf which he'd been fattening up for Passover. Then Mother bathed my feet and dried them gently with her hair. Most odd behaviour!

Eventually, when they'd calmed down a bit, their attention wandered outside and thereupon settled upon Jim, my brother,

45

standing sulkily in the road. Overjoyed, I watched them rush out, to greet him (or so I thought). Imagine my dismay, however, when they both set about him like whirling dervishes telling him never to darken their doorstep again. Dad then rushed back within the house, grabbed a handful of coins, flew out, kicked him firmly up the backside and then threw him and the money into the gutter.

Knowing my parents, however, I was fairly sure they couldn't stay that mad for long, so I confidently expected them to change their minds before nightfall.

Later on that evening, there was a huge, somewhat embarrassing, feast to celebrate my return. Never one to miss a party and a free meal, I noticed my bad, banished brother Jim skulking about in the background wearing a ridiculous false moustache, eyeing up the girls and getting drunk as a skunk. When the party was over, several guests noticed that some of their possessions had been nicked and, moreover, one particularly irate chap found his new sports camel, that he'd parked outside, had been hijacked.

Ah well, as it sayeth in the Book of Kings, 'As a dog returneth to his vomit, so a fool returneth to his folly!'

In the fullness of time, Jim came sheepishly back and his parents grudgingly let him stay, but he was always to be a thorn in their side, as you will see in future extracts. Mind you, it must have been a bit of a strain having someone as perfect as Jesus as your brother.*

It is reported in Luke that, much later, Jesus used the story as an example to his followers. In the Parable of the Prodigal Son, however, he cunningly switched the ending. In his rendition, the naughty lad returned home, after blowing all his money on wine and women, of his own volition. His father, unlike Joseph, welcomed him with open arms, forgiving him instantly. That night, similarly, there was a huge celebration feast (fatted calf and all) in his honour, but in this story, his brother (Jesus's equivalent) was well miffed at the treatment the bad brother was getting, as *he'd* stayed at home and had served his father perfectly all the time, and hadn't had as much as a Chicken McNugget in *his* honour.

* Far from going down the slippery slope to eternal damnation, Jim, realizing what a total prat he'd been, went away and started, in his twenties, to get his act together. He was eventually murdered by a Sadducee (a sect like the Pharisees) in 62 AD and was thought to have written his own gospel, found in Nag Hammedi in 1945. He is now known as James the Righteous.

Jesus and the Whale

When Jesus was nearly sixteen, he suddenly got it in to his head that he wanted to go to sea as a fisherman. He'd done a little fishing earlier with his dad (see page 19), and had been rather successful (albeit with a little help from God). But apart from that, he'd always loved the ocean and, anyway, was becoming well bored with churning out oxen yolks, milking stools, seed drills and all things wooden in his father's workshop. He craved to see more of the world and, if he became at home on the high seas, he would become a proper sailor on a huge merchant ship which would travel the length and breadth of the known world (and, with a bit of luck, a few more places to boot).

1st December 12 AD

Today was my day off from the wood business, so instead of going forth to the synagogue to gabble scripture with the old men, as per usual, I awoke real early and walked for several hours over to the fishing village just south of ACCO on the banks of the Great Sea. I made sure I travelled before the sun got hot enough to fry your brains, but lo, by the time I hit the harbour, all the brightly painted, high prowed boats were parked up, and the rather knackered looking fishermen, who'd been out a-fishing all night, were lounging about, sipping mint tea, spitting, smoking and gambling. The nets had been hung out to dry and all the fish that wasn't destined for local markets, had been salted and boxed ready to be sent forth to Jerusalem and even further flung parts of the Romans' enormous empire (and may it giv'em gut-ache!).

'I say my good men! How went last night's catch?' I casually asked a group of old sea dogs who, completely ignoring me, carried on throwing dice upon the sand. 'Where dost one find out about a career at sea?' I persisted.

They all spat, looked up and then one of them replied in a rather rough, uncultured voice. 'Get lost sonny. Go play with your TOY boats. Fishing's for men not kids.'

'Why can't I become a fisherman? I'm fifteen and, verily, not the least bit a-feared of the sea,' I replied, slightly put out by their rudeness.

And lo, they all nearly laughed their beards off, in a most crude manner, then spat again, and carried on with their game as if I wasn't even there.

'Who should I speak unto if I want to have a go,' I shouted.

'Me,' croaked the oldest man, who looked as if he was made of worn-out cow-hide and who spat right betwixt my feet. 'If thou really wants to come with us, be here at eleven sharp tonight, but don't expect no favours, we're not running a flippin' pleasure boat for time-wasters you know.'

Then they all spat in unison and carried on.

2nd December 12 AD

Lordie, what a night! I canst hardly tell you . . . but I'll have a go.

I crept out of the house last night at about ten of the clock, when my family were safely within their beds, and ran nearly all the way to the coast. As I turned up, the boats bobbed upon the water with their sails unfurled, just about to set off but, verily, the old leather-man honoured his word and let me join them. I might have guessed: as soon as I was aboard the stinking vessel, the other men instantly started taking the mickey, calling me a wimp and proclaiming that I'd be more use as bait.

Look, I'm no prude, but their conversation (for want of a better word) was by far the filthiest that ever I've heard. Such blaspheming! Twas as much as I couldst do not to tell them the error of their ways.

After about an hour or so had passed, they dropped their nets over the side and drifted. The surly sailors sang obscene sea-shanties about well-endowed and willing wenches a-shore, and puffed noisily on their disgusting pipes, sending up clouds of smoke that would have choked any seabird misguided enough to fly nearby, while they waited to come upon a shoal of fishes.

And it came to pass that their cussing and blaspheming became worse and worse, and verily, they were taking my Lord's name in vain to such a degree that I simply HAD to warn them of His fearful wrath if they didn't belt up. This set them off again, as they thought my outburst hilarious. But lo, the fishermen eventually got well fed up with my protestations and ordered me upon the very top of the rigging to look out for any signs of fish a-jumping upon the water.

I had been stuck up there maybe half an hour when — shock horror! I spied, far in the distance, what looked to be a huge and monstrous tail, the height of a house, rearing from the water and then a mighty

black shape coming straight for us real fast, cutting a deep path through the swell and causing a massive wake either side.

'Whale ahoy.' I cried in sheer terror. 'WHALE AHOY!!'

All the fishermen spat, looked up; then looked upon each other; and then, couldst thou believe, fell upon each other sobbing with laughter. Never, in all their years at sea, they cried, had a whale been seen in these waters, and no one ever said 'AHOY!' any more. Anyway, they added scornfully, they certainly weren't going to believe the screams and anguish of some wet-behind-the-ears nipper who was probably dreaming on account of being up well past his bedtime.

'Of course there's a whale,' yelled the old man sarcastically, without even a-spying in the direction of my pointing.' Tell you what, young whipper-snapper. Why dost thou not tie the beast to the prow of the blasted boat, then we'll get along famously?

The other fishermen fell upon each other laughing as though it were the funniest thing they'd ever heard in their entire lives.

And lo, suddenly, with an ear-shattering, timber-tearing C-RUNCH, the mighty beast smited the boat amidships, with an impact that sent the men sprawling onto their faces, amongst the slimy fish heads and old nets. I, on the other hand, was tossed high into the air, where I seemed to hang for a few seconds (which I spent rather usefully — fervently praying to God) before plummeting into the inky black depths of the ocean.

51

By the time I broketh the surface, the boat was a long way in the distance, listing badly. I, fortunately, came upon the very severed spar upon which I'd been sitting when on high, and clung on for dear life. Luckily the old H_2O was quite warm so, apart from the danger of savage sharks, sinister sea serpents and, of course that blasted whale, I only had to hang on and wait for the others to come back and find me (if and when they'd noticed me gone).

But I hung on throughout the rest of the night and when the sun rose, the darned fishing boat was nowhere to be seen. But, twas my good fortune, yet again, that the current had carried me towards the land, so I paddled with my legs and lo, after half an hour, found myself sprawled upon a long sandy beach, amongst all the fish heads and slime, that had washed off the boat when the whale struck.

At first it appeared to be deserted, but when I'd dried off and was about to set off homeward, an old woman happened by, collecting driftwood for her cooking fire. She told me that she had just cometh hence from the fishing village where everyone was yacking, nineteen to the dozen, about the appalling events of the night before. Apparently, she said, some monstrous whale had smitten one of the local boats and swallowed a poor lad who had only gone along for the ride. The villagers were now smitten with terror as to what form the Lord's revenge might take. Even the boy's parents had cometh to the village, she said, as they hath seemed to know instinctively that it was their son that had been gobbled up.

'But why should the Lord take revenge?' I enquired innocently, as I realized the old crone hadn't put two-and-two together and realized that I was the one they were looking for. She then sighed deeply, squatted on the sand and began the Old Testament tale in which some guy called Jonah had suffered a similar fate whale-wise.

And this is the story she told.

Apparently, once upon a time, in ancient Nineveh, the capital (and fleshpot) of the mighty Assyrian Empire, the depravity of the people had got to such a high level, or low (depending on which way you look upon it), that God became mighty miffed.

Now this fellow Jonah was a professional prophet, by all accounts, so God ordered him to get propheting and make his way to the sinful city to tell the king and his subjects, in words of one syllable, to clean up their act. Otherwise He wouldst do something extremely horrid to them. Now, Jonah, it happened, didn't mind telling his fellow Jews what to do but didn't really relish pitching up to some strange palace, in some strange city, in order to tell the boss of one of the

52

most bloodthirsty nations in the world how he should run his and his people's lives (and who canst blame him?).

Straightaway he jumped, therefore, upon a merchant ship bound for Tarshish (a place that nobody up Israel way had even heard of) which was, surprise, surprise, in completely the opposite direction to Nineveh. Jonah obviously thought, silly fool, that he could escape from God.

The old lady rambled on to describe how God became almost as hacked off with Jonah as he'd been with all those filthy folk of fun-filled Nineveh, and sent forthwith a huge gale to sink the ship that he'd taken and was now within — below decks — snoring. All the terrified sailors, realizing this was no run-of-the-mill storm asked each other, and even drew lots, to see who it was that the Lord had it in for. Jonah, being the silly twerp that he was, crawled up upon deck and, half in sleep, let slip that he was actually, at that moment in time, in the process of disobeying God's orders and so, verily, there was a fair chance that it was him that the Lord was trying to zap.

The poor sailors soon sussed that, if they didn't chuck Jonah overboard, they'd all perish too, so apologizing profusely (as one should), they pushed him over the edge and, believe it or not, straight away the winds subsided and they were saved. All, of course, except Jonah (as thou might have guessed) who was, poor geezer, now approaching dead deep trub in more ways than one. If it wasn't bad enough floating around miles from nowhere without so much as water wings,* God had yet another nasty trick up his voluminous sleeve.

* Not invented yet.

'Behold a mighty fish, called a whale, came forth and gobbled him up,' the old woman cried, nearly deafening me.

Now I should have told her that, in truth, a whale is a mammal and not a fish, and moreover there was no way that it couldst swallow a human being, on account of its weeny throat, but felt that this might be thought to be splitting hairs at this juncture.

'Anyway,' she continued, 'he sat around inside this horrid smelly fish, a-twiddling his thumbs, for three whole days before the somewhat uncouth beast burped (owing to severe indigestion, methinks) and spat him out, right as rain, close to a beach. As soon as he was dry, God told him to get down Nineveh way real pronto, and do what he was supposed to do the first time, which is exactly what he did. But really I couldn't see the connection. After all, Jonah had been disobeying direct orders from God. Whereas I had simply been involved in an everyday whale-hits-boat accident. Still, it did seem rather a coincidence that the two stories were similar. Once again I felt mighty confused. Was God trying to tell me something. And if so – what?

I thanked the old lady kindly and asked which way to the village (let's face it there could only be a choice of two) and set off upon the sand with some apprehension. Would the assembled throng set upon me for causing them so much anguish and fear? Would my parents knock the living daylights from me for leaving home without a word? Or would they all laugh at me for being so stupid?

As I rounded the bay, I heard mass wailing (as opposed to whaling) and saw, in the distance, hordes of people a-crying, a-tearing of their clothes and donning sackcloth (all the rage in the guilt business). Suddenly my mother, always guaranteed to be the most theatrical, spotted me and, turning pale, fell upon the ground crying louder than anyone else. It was only then that I realized how I must have looked and smelt. I was still covered in a horrid mixture of seaweed, sand and fish scales and lo, smelt like an old fishmonger's apron (or the inside of a whale no less!).

'Jesus, Jesus!' she cried. 'You are saved from the belly of the mighty whale. Hallelujah! Hallelujah! Praise the Lord.'

The others all repeated the hallelujahs at the tops of their voices, and fell at my feet as if I had done something brave and wonderful.

'Listen you lot, I haven't been in any wh . . .' I attempted to say. 'Maybe a—'

But the howling and praise-the-Lording drowned out my protestations.

Then the horrid old fisherman, who had captained the boat, flung himself in front of me and grovelled in a most disgusting manner.

'Oh master, tell God that we meant not all those terrible things we said about Him on the boat last night. Tell Him that we will change our ways, pray lots and go forth to the synagogue every sabbath. Tell Him that we won't swear or sing bawdy songs about women's rude bits. Tell Him how truly remorseful we really are about the way we treated you.'

'I'm sure I don't have to tell him,' I replied. 'The Lord is with us all the time and can hear every word.'

With that they all looked to the sky and fell crying upon their knees again promising to reform over and over.

Look Lord, I knowest I could have put a bit more effort into convincing them that I hadn'st ever been fish-food, and I know that I'm probably going to dine out for months on the tale of what it was like to be swallowed and live within the stomach of a whale, but the way I see it, all that throng have changed greatly for the better. If it hadn't been for the old inside-whale bit of the yarn, they might not have made the Jonah connection and, thereupon, taken it all so seriously.

Jesus and Girls

Jesus was now sixteen, and a very attractive lad; in a rather gentle, non-macho, kind of way. His pleasing features, plus his warm, help-anyone-at-any-time personality had made him a firm favourite with all the adolescent girls at school – and quite a lot of the old girls in the village, too. But, more than all this, he came over as dead *cool*, appearing to be not the least bit interested in the opposite sex (or his own!) which, as you can imagine, made him a thousand times more fascinating than all his leering, suggestive, and often just plain rude, male contemporaries.

His mother, Mary, had a bit of a dilemma (yet again). She had always known he was somewhat special; not surprising when one remembers his somewhat bizarre conception and the fuss surrounding his actual birth. One side of her loved the fact that the apple of her eye appeared to be above all that rather tacky sex business, but on the other hand, she'd always wanted a daughter-in-law; not only to gossip about the menfolk with, but also to help with the daily chores. Most Jewish families of the period tended to stick together (dad simply tacked on an extra bit to the existing house), so a marriage in the family would not only

mean another woman in the home, but with a bit of luck, an imminent hoard of grubby, snotty grand-children scurrying around for her to shout at.

Both her and hubby Joseph were pretty sure that Jesus's nere-do-well brother Jim would never donate anything meaningful to the family tree, and judging by the decidedly dodgy young ladies he'd already knocked around with, they felt confident in the knowledge that if he did eventually get hitched (due to a black-mailing parent no doubt), they would be bound to disapprove of his choice.

Jesus, it must be said, kept the whole subject of his personal attitude to maidens very close to his chest. He was well aware of their attractions but had never even kissed a girl and hadn't a clue what was expected of him (if anything).

2nd March 13 AD

Oh Lord, how can I handle all this weird boy/girl business? Everybody I know grilleth me about when it will come to pass that I will eventually succumb to girlish charms. For a start, there's my old lady who insisteth on dragging my dreadful cousin Joanna round (the one with the buck teeth) and leaving her with me, like a filly at a stud farm. It wouldn't be quite so bad if she didn't spit when she spake. Verily, after an hour with her, one's soaked from head to foot.

Then there's Mrs Elijahson, up the road, who keeps yanking me in for a mint tea with her vast daughter Eloise, who is very much upon the (very much sagging) shelf. Verily Lord, she seems nice enough if you're into the sort of thing they use to test the strength of donkeys, but if she ever got her hands on yours truly, she'd crush the living daylights from out of me. Lordie! What a dreadful way to go.

But they're just the obvious non-runners. Why canst people understand that I'm not at all sure that girls, marriage and eventually nippers are to be on my agenda ever?

Much, much worse than all this, however, is the ever more appalling sitch at school. Only this very day, on the way home, I was waylaid by Rebecca and Ruth (the dynamic duo), who offered me some private biology practical if I was to go forth with them behind the goat-sheds. I sometimes think there might be some sort of wager amongst the local girls, to see who can go out with me first - very flattering, but a bit scary.

Woe is me. If only I couldst persuade them that even if I did, some time in the distant future, succumb to their well-advertised charms, I'm not at all sure. I'd have a clue what I should do. Why didnst my parents tell me all the facts of life. Verily, I have witnessed all the beasts in the fields at it, and the birds and fishes, but I can't imagine being able to keep a straight face if it ever happened to me. As for Mum and Dad. . . .

Perchance I'll go forth to the synagogue and ask the old men how I should handle this whole prob.

3rd March 13 AD

Well that's really gone and done it. Young Jemima (the school flirt) accosted me after lessons and told me slyly that she needed my help.

'Hi, Jesus, I wondered if I might ask thou to sit down with me for a few minutes. I've got a bit of a problem with my school work? I'd be EVER SO grateful.'

'Of course, Jemima,' sayeth I, fearing some ulterior motive and flushing upon my cheeks. 'If I can be of any assistance, I'd be only too happy to oblige. Which subject struggleth thou with?'

'Oh, it's just all that stuff about the birds and the bees that we talked about today,' she replied. 'There's a few things I can't understand. Thou art so learned, and so helpful, I'm sure you could clear up a few questions for me.'

Oh no, I thought. Here we go again. Another fine mess I'm about to get myself into. The trouble is this, Jemima just never takes nay for an answer.

'You see it's just that I don't understand how a man . . . er . . . I mean male, of any species, knows what to do when . . . well you know,' she said.

'Well er . . . um . . . it's l-like . . . er . . . this,' I stuttered. 'The male of the species . . . er . . . m-must . . . er . . . sort of . . . well . . . k-kind of . . . Surely its all in your notes.'

'It mentions where, why and the results,' she giggled, 'but it doesn't actually say how.' Her hand now touched my cheek, and I felt myself beginning to overheat like a polar bear on a beach.

'Well,' I croaked, my mind racing like it was the very devil's inquisition, 'it's different for everyone, I mean . . . er, for all the multitude of species. Birds do it one way, bees do it another, elepha—'

'But how do we do it, Jesus?' she whispered.

'We? You mean us humans?' I squeeked (my mind racing going into turbo-charge), 'Oh I . . . er . . . well . . . let me see . . . first of all we . . . er . . . go and ask our mothers.'

With that I mumbled something about having to help my dad in the workshop and tore off down the path that ran by our school. I turned round briefly to see Jemima sitting open-mouthed, exactly where I'd left her.

Verily, I must see the rabbis tomorrow without fail, before this whole business getteth well out of hand.

4th March 13 AD

I've just returned from a long session with the elders, and I must admit I'm somewhat more confused than before. I had told them that I felteth a certain amount of pressure as round these parts it's not uncommon for kids to be married as early as nine years of age (heaven forbid!). Indeed, the average age for fatherhood is 19, grandfatherhood, 38 and, would'st thou believest, great-grandfatherhood, 57. More to the point, parents often favoureth marriage betwixt first cousins (which might just account for the number of loopy kids at school!).

The first thing the rabbis told me was that, despite all that stuff, I shouldn't worry too much about the immediacy of the problem. After all Abraham was still fathering nippers at 100 years old, and some of those old rogues went on even longer. Adam, who started the whole ball rolling, fathered young Seth at 130, which must have been a touch traumatic experience, as he waited 800 hundred years to have another (by which time I reckon poor old Eve must have looked somewhat long in the tooth). Moreover, that crafty old Noah (of 'ark' fame) had his three boys Shem, Ham and Japheth when merely middle-aged, at around 500. Apparently women went on a bit longer too, in ancient days. They told me that Sarah, Isaac's mum, had him when she was 90. Not bad! I reckon the fact that she and Abraham still fancied each-other must count for something. I wonder if Mum and Dad will still . . . ?

Next I asked them to give unto me the lowdown on whether I HAD to be married to have anything to do with girls? The old men dived straight into The Book of Deutoronomy from whence they came up with the following, rather hair-raising, warning.

You must, they read, check fairly carefully, for a start, that the object of your affection is not already married or even engaged . . . otherwise thou could well find thyself stoned to death at the nearest town gate – as well as thy new sweet-heart. That seemeth a bit final, but fairly straightforward, I thought. Then, apparently, if thou meeteth a maid that isn't hitched up, but, notwithstanding, you force her to lie with you before marriage, you must give her dad fifty pieces of silver and then marry her (I could see unscrupulous, money-grabbing fathers getting quite a bit of mileage out of that one). By the by, If you've been careless enough to have thy testicles crushed or your willy severed assunder, not only can you not get married, but according to the law, you can't become a member of the Assembly of the Lord either.

I'VE GOT PLENTY MORE WHERE SHE CAME FROM

They continued: Quite a good way of finding a wife occurs if you manage, when in war mode, to capture all your enemies – male and female. Apparently, it says; if amongst them there's a lady you really fancyeth, you can take her home with you and treat her as a wife, on condition – that is – that you shaveth her head (which could lessen her appeal somewhat), cut her nails, and then burn all her clothes (which could increase her appeal somewhat). Then, it states, you must wait a month while she recovereth from the loss of her mum and dad (and hair, nails and clothes), and then, only then, can you sleep with her. If, after a bit, you changeth your mind, it goes on to say:

And it shall be, if thou has no delight in her, then you shalt let her go whither she will: But thou shalt not sell her at all for money.

– which I think soundeth more than reasonable. You can't just go round selling off your ex-conquests (or wives). Women, on the other hand, are stuck with their husbands, and are not allowed to leave (though I've heard the Romans are now trying to rectify that).

So it all looketh fairly conclusive that sex outside the sanctity of marriage is a bit of a no-no. Some of the old timers, notwithstanding, obviously got round this problem fairly neatly. After all, it's well

61

documented that old King Solomon had 700 wives, and when he became fed up with that lot, was allowed 300 concubines (one of the perks of the job perchance).

Before I could even ask of them the next question, one of the rabbis waved his finger and warned that it sayeth in *The Book of Genesis* that spilling one's seed upon the ground is, '**a sin unto the Lord and punishable by DEATH!**'

And they wonder why I want to leave this whole man/woman business alone.

Jesus the Doctor

Like all good mothers, Mary always had a bit of a hankering for her son Jesus to become a doctor. She knew that he was somewhat special and that God probably had big plans for him, but thought that 'saviouring', as such, left a lot to be desired security-wise. Jesus was not that sure. Anyway, if the early scriptures were anything to go by, medicine, in those days, was dodgy to say the least, being heavily linked to superstition and magic (often black).

For example, if you were a little whacky in the old brain department, you could forget any sort of drug treatment, let alone therapy. You were simply regarded as having a '*roof demon*' so named after the evil spirits that, if you'd been a touch unlucky as a baby, were thought to slide down the roof, jump through the window and squeeze into your head. Instead of going to a doctor for treatment, your mum and dad would ring an exorcist (a skill our Jesus was to learn later – (see page 29).

Here's another example. In order to prevent miscarriages in biblical times, it was common practice for the lady in question to wrap a dead scorpion in crocus green cloth and pin it to her skirt (don't even ask!). Or, to guarantee an easy birth, women would drink powdered ivory in strong wine. When the, no doubt, tipsy nipper was born, it had to suffer being rubbed all over with salt and then being imprisoned in tight bindings (called swaddling clothes) due to the totally whacky idea that movement was bad for their little limbs.

Let's have a peep at Jesus's diary when he decides to look a little closer into the health business.

13th April 13 AD

Dear Diary

Verily, I love, honour and respect Mary that is my mother, but if she doesn't stop droning on about my being a doctor, I think I shalt soon need one myself. I've told her that God might well have other ideas but will she listen? Will she heck! Today I decided to go forth to the synagogue and consult the scriptures to see what this medical stuff involves.

And lo, after explaining the sitch to the elders, they told me that even in ancient days it looked as if the men of God didst most of the medical work. I must say it all soundeth a bit hit and miss.

Take leprosy, for instance. I'd always thought that it was one of those diseases that you treateth with a bit of respect, especially as, if you didn't, there was a fair chance that crucial bits (noses, ears, toes and much, much worse!) would start departing from your body at an alarming rate. In the ancient Book of Leviticus, however, Moses (who wrote it with God's help) seemed to have been a touch confused.

When the plague of leprosy is in a man, then he shall be brought unto the priest; and the priest shall see him; and behold if the rising be white in the skin, and it has turned the hair white, and there be quick raw flesh in the rising; it is an old leprosy in the skin of his flesh and the priest shall pronounce him unclean, and shall not shut him up for he is unclean.

(OK mate, we get the message!)
Now that seemeth fairly reasonable. The guy hath leprosy, so there's no point banging him up away from his leper mates. The next bit, however, hath me well puzzled:

And if the leprosy break out abroad in the skin, and the leprosy cover all the skin of him that hath the plague from his head even to his foot wheresoever the priest looketh; then the priest shall consider: and, behold, if the leprosy hath covered all his flesh, he shall pronounce him clean that hath the plague: it is all turned white: he is clean.

Now surely that must mean that if he's got just a bit of leprosy he's unclean, but if he's got the whole blinking lot he's reckoned to be fine.
Well, that's leprosy for you. Here's a weird one. What about if a chap goes to the priest suffering from an itchy head and hair loss? Leviticus says:

And the man whose hair has fallen off his head, he is bald; yet he is clean (And why not?)
And he that has his hair fallen off from the part of his head that is towards his face, he is forehead bald (brilliant!): yet he is clean.

But if there be in the bald head a white, reddish sore: it is leprosy ... He is unclean ... And the leper in whom the plague is, his clothes shall be rent (torn) and his head bare, and he shall put a covering on his upper lip, and shall cry, 'Unclean, unclean.'

Oh no! If it's not bad enough having such a dire disease (and a follicly challenged head) they want you to grow a moustache as well.

But lo, it was no fun being without hair in those days. In the Second Book of Kings, Elisha, a well known bald person of the time, was on his way to Bethel when a host of little city kids ran up and shouteth: **'Go up; thou bald head, go up; thou bald head!'**

He got his revenge, however, even if it was a bit excessive. It appears that old baldie turned round and cursed them in the name of God, whereupon two she-bears appeared on the scene, as if by magic, and slew 42 of the little blighters. Honestly, some people just can't taketh a joke.

14th April 13 AD

I've just discovered the beginnings of a horrid swelling upon my neck. I suppose I should go to see someone about it. But, dear Father above, I keep remembering old Job, the famous sayer of psalms, when he was feeling a touch under the weather, saying to the Lord: **'Because of your wrath there is no health in my body; my bones have no soundness because of my sin.'**

So I suppose that must mean that I'VE done something that offendeth the Lord though, for the life of me, I can't think what it can be. Moreover, I don't want some priest telling me I have leprosy. Even so, I decided to go down to the synagogue again to see if the scriptures could offer any cure. I really should have known better.

The elders really put the wind up me today. They read to me a few lines from Exodus about when God told Moses to go and see the Pharaoh and tell him that if he didn't let his people make sacrifices to Him, he could expect something dead nasty. When the Pharaoh refused, Moses instructed the old man to throw handfuls of soot into the air, right in front of him, so that, with a bit of luck (and the wind in the right direction), it would spread over the whole of Egypt (and not turn him black!). This, apparently, came to pass and, because of this accursed soot, every living thing was covered in horrible open boils.

Now as far as I can remember, I haven't been near any soot for ages, so I doubt if it can be that. Nor have I been remotely near the Ark* of the Covenant which also, it is said, causes piles and boils, if tampered with by any unauthorized person or persons.

Verily, I was still at a loss to discover the cause and treatment for my ever-enlarging eruption, which was sore vexing me, to say the least. Then one of the rabbis found a passage in 2 Kings which described a time 700 years ago when Hezekiah, one of Isaiah's

* (Arks in ancient days were either small, like the one holding God's laws on tablets of stone, or somewhat larger, like the one that old nutter called Noah built as a floating zoo (see page 96).

sort of patients (and King of Judah for a living) was dying from a huge swelling somewhere upon his nether regions. Then God spake unto Isaiah telling him to give him another fifteen years life by applying a poultice of figs to his mountainous boil.

I rushed back home and asked our neighbour Mr Jeremiahson, who's got a big fig tree in his back yard, if I could have some (I didn't want to incur any more of God's wrath by scrumping). He found it all a bit strange, but gave me a basketfull all the same. I mashed them up and strapped them upon my neck with a piece of fine muslin.

18th April 13 AD

The poultice has been on several days now, and all goeth well till this morning. The boil was well reduced, and lo, I was feeling much better. The figs were beginning to go rotten, however, and the village folk were giving me strange looks as I reeketh not a little. Verily, as I was about to remove the damn thing, Mum asked me to go out to relieve the goats and then tend to the hives (essential in a land of milk and honey). Just as I came upon the first hive, the little b's caught wind of me (or should I say the stinking figs) and rushed within to tell their numerous mates. Suddenly they arose as one bee and swarmed out, settling upon me. I tore round the back yard flailing at them to no good avail, and eventually dived into the water butt. But lo, when I emerged, I was covered from head to foot in horrid red stings. As the old saying from The Book of Acts goes 'it **is hard for thee to kick against the pricks'** which, I think, refers to that sort of situation.

22nd April 13 AD

Meanwhile, back to doctoring. Having had no great fortune finding out any proper medical knowledge from the scriptures, I strolled over to Sepphoris our nearest biggish town, to check up on the local physician-cum-surgeon. Many years past, the rabbis had decreed that every town must have at least one, and that in order to charge money, they must be licensed by them.

Lo, I found the shop, or should I say surgery, in question in a dingy back street with a peeling sign that proclaimed:

Z. ZACHARIAS-LICENSED PHYSICIAN AND SURGEON
ALL KNOWN AILMENTS CURED AT REASONABLE COST
MINOR SURGERY PERFORMED WHILE-U-WAIT

On entering, I was amazed to find the place in a state of total disarray, with bottles, pill boxes, baskets of herbs, surgical instruments and jars containing pickled parts of unidentifiable beasts covering every inch of the floor, walls, counters and chairs. On the shelves were crammed thousands of dusty scrolls and manuscripts. In the midst of all this chaos sat an old white-haired man wearing a skull-cap, who appeared to be trying to assemble a rather grubby skeleton which must have fallen to pieces and now resembled a jigsaw.

When he heard the tinkle from the little bell above the door, he looked up and regarded me over his little gold glasses. 'Yes, young man. Can'st I be of some assistance to you?' he wheezed in a thin piping voice. 'Thou art lucky, I've only just opened.'

'I'm truly sorry,' I replied, viewing the chaos. 'I seemeth to have come at a rather inconvenient time. Hast thou just been burgled?'

'Burgled! What dost thou mean, burgled?' he replied, looking round in some puzzlement. 'I've only just finished tidying up.'

'Oh, I just thought . . .'

'What canst I do for you?' he repeated in a rather tetchy manner. 'Can't you see I'm a busy man. I'm just trying to assemble my dear father's bones.'

'Well, it's like this. My mother wouldst like for me to be a doctor, and I just desireth to see what's involved. Is there very much to learn?'

'Much to learn? Much to learn?' he cried. 'I'll say there's much to learn, young man. Verily, it hath taken all my working life to know what I know.'

'I just wondered if I might sit quietly in the corner for a few hours and observe how thou goest about daily work. It might help me to decide whether I want to do doctoring for a living.'

He looked round shiftily but grudgingly agreed and, without further ado, I sat myself down in the corner and waited. After a short time, customers began to come forth. They were a motley crew, suffering from everything from sore throats, headaches and rashes to rheumatism, acne and severe colds.

And lo, each time the old doctor wouldst listen, rather impatiently, to their complaints, and then go to the shelves and hunt around, in a cloud of dust, for the appropriate scroll, which he wouldst pore over until appearing to find the right remedy. He would then disappear into a little back room from which one couldst hear the sounds of bottles being uncorked, liquids being poured and potions being stirred. After some time, he would emerge and direct the customer as to how they should take or apply the potions or lotions. Then, with much glee, he would tell them the price and relieve them of their cash.

I couldn't help noticing, however, that each time he went forth to the back room the sounds were almost identical, as was the time taken. By moving to the right, a cubit or so, I found that I could view exactly what he was doing by watching his reflection within a small mirror that hung upon the opposite wall.

Lo and behold, when he went to mix the medicine for the next customer, I watched the old rogue make uncorking noises with his thumb over an empty vessel, pour what looketh like water, betwixt one jug to another, and make loud stirring noises using a spoon in an empty cup. Then, fully believing that he wasn't being observed, he

70

dippeth a spoon into a huge pot which said HRRYM on the front, and mixed it with olive oil and what appeareth to be a little colouring. He thenceforth decanted this mixture into one of a 100 or so little pots. This same procedure he repeated for every punter, only changing the colouring each time. Verily, I surmised that either the old guy was a phoney or this HRRYM stuff cureth all ills.

Since then I've asked everyone I know whether they've heard of it, but have drawneth a complete blank.

23rd April 13 AD

And it came to pass, that just as I was beginning to go off the idea of being a medic, my mate Ishmael rushed in with his pet puppy Gog, who'd just been attacked by some wild beast up in the hills. There was a nasty gash in the poor little bitch's (sorry Lord!) side and she was bleeding awfully. I asked him if he'd heard of this stuff called HRRYM as I thought it might do the trick. He asked me to write it down and, blow me, just as I turned it round so that he could read it, I happened to view it upside down. This new word MYRRH rang a distant bell in my brain and I remembered that, some time ago, the priests had been banging on about the healing properties of this incredibly rare resin from some obscure African tree.

Suddenly it dawned upon me that I had read the label in the doctor's shop back-to-front through the mirror, and that it had been MYHRR all the time that he used.

When I returned home, I casually asked Mum if, by any chance, we had any in the house. She gave me a strange, knowing look and then quizzed me as to what I wanted it for. When I told her, she slipped out to the carpentry shop and whispered with Joseph my father, for quite some time. He then went to a mysterious ancient locked chest that had always been in their bedroom and brought out this wondrous, pretty pot which looked as if it was made from purest gold. He reluctantly gave it unto me saying that some rich stranger, who'd said he was some sort of noble relative, had brought it forth as a present when I was born. He told me that he'd intended giving it to me as a kind of surprise, with a couple of other goodies, when I reached 21.

I ran out the back with the pot to where Gog was now in a bit of a state. Having cut away the surrounding fur, I shoved some of the sticky stuff upon her wound, praying to God that it would work. All we could do now was wait and pray a bit more.

26th April 13 AD

I awoke early to find an amazed and delighted Ishmael at my front door. Apparently he'd peeked under Gog's bandage at cock-crow and got the shock of his life to find, not only the bleeding to have stopped, but the cut to have completely disappeared and all the fur to have grown back. Crikey! I thought, this myrrh is the real biz, I'd better keepeth it somewhere safe.

30th April 13 AD

Lordie, what a weird few days! It had come to pass, on the day of Gog's miraculous recovery, that a local shepherd of sheep turned up with a sickly lamb that looked due to meet its mint sauce. The poor thing could hardly stand, and stood shivering pathetically upon the doorstep. I told its owner that I wasn't a proper physician, but didn't mind having a go. Apparently the whole village was talking about Gog's wondrous recovery and so this guy had come to see if there was anything I couldst do with his poor little bleater.

   I crept out the back, forthwith, and got the old myrrh out again. This time I mixeth some up with an equal quantity of olive oil and poureth it down the little varmint's throat. I then prayed to my Lord, as before, and lo, almost before my very eyes, can you believe it? The little thing stopped shaking, bounced a foot in the air and frolicked off up the road at a fair rate. The shepherd stared upon

ANXIOUS MUM

me, then at the lively lamb, then upon me again. He backed away nervously, hardly even able to thank me for getting his lamb sheep-shape again.

The following morning, I woke to sounds of barking, lowing, baaing, tweeting, miaowing and ee-awing, and when I looked out of the window I saw a smallish multitude, stretching yonder down the road, of people I'd hardly seen before, with an assortment of animals from cats to camels, finches to falcons and gudgeon to goldfish.

One by one, I treated the various creatures; either slapping my trusty myrrh directly on the wounds if they were injured, or mixing it with the olive oil and shoving it down their assorted throats and beaks if they were simply poorly. Out of nearly fifty animals, every one was miraculously cured! All, that is, except a poor old donkey called Habakkuk, who belonged to Obediah the peddlar who, after having swallowed the medicine, simply keeled over and died, legs akimbo.

Last night, I went back over the procedure to find out why the silly ass had died and realized that the only thing that I'd forgotten to do was pray to the Lord while treating him. Pure coincidence I thought.

3rd May 13 AD

By now everyone was talking about my talents as a healer, and they all wanted to know my secret. I supposeth I'm a bit naughty, but I decided to keep it to myself as I'm really enjoying being able to help people and their pets. Anyway, it will soon all be over, as I have reached the last scrapings of the myrrh pot. I tried to explain to some guy whose camel hath humps – sorry – mumps but, because I hadn't told anyone what I'd been using, he, like them, had supposed I'd used a whole cabinet full of potions and drugs to sort out the various ailments.

There was nothing for it. I either had to confess my secret, or carry on until they realized I'd lost my knack and so leave me alone. With great trepidation, I poured olive oil (coloured with fig juice) straight from the golden pot, down the throat of the camel, praying silently unto God and then waited. And it came to pass, after ten terribly long seconds, the camel belcheth, stood up, and then calmly loped off – fit as a fiddle.

This time the multitude weren't that surprised, but I certainly was. It wasn't the myrrh after all, and it couldn't be the oil, as I

hadn't been using that on wounds. In a blinding flash, it dawned on me. Of course, it could only be the gold pot from the guy who soundeth a bit of a wizard, who'd pitched up when I was a nipper. Whatever it contained obviously took on healing qualities.

4th May 13 AD

Well, it really is all over this time. At about midday, after I'd treated some fifty animals, I was about to close for lunch, when I decided to slip off for a pee before closing for an hour. Lo, while I was away, some ungrateful so-and-so crept in and nicked my precious gold pot. I, therefore, think I'd better call it a day as there's no way I can do it without the enchanted pot (let alone the myrrh). Hey ho, t'was fun while it lasted.

Jesus hadn't realized that it was God who had given him these mighty healing powers, and the old doctor of Sepphoris was after all, a right fraudster. For years he went on believing it was due to the myrrh or the gold pot that had been given to his parents by the Wise Men.

Jesus and the Law

Mary was a bit disappointed when her son decided that the medical profession was not really for him, but being highly ambitious for her offspring (well, with the exception of Jesus's brother Jim), and not being one to fall at the first fence, she set her mind on the other prestigious profession – the law. She then went on and on at Jesus to look into it. Jesus, on the other hand, had never relished the idea of a desk job (as desks as such hadn't been invented), but promised his mum he wouldn't dismiss it without finding out a bit more.

12th July 13 AD

Dear Diary

I decided this very morning that I'd do a bit of research to keep the old lady happy. Now that Herod Archelaus (horrid Herod's stupid son) has been kicked out by the Romans, it means that us Jews must, henceforth, answer to them if we do anything real naughty. Upon the other hand, there are all the rules relating to being a good Jew that were set down by God and also, all the dreadful things that could come to pass if one disobeyed. I went forthwith to the synagogue and asked the elders if they could let me go through the relevent scriptures to find out exactly what's what within the Old Testament. They directed me straightaway to the commandments put down by the mighty Moses (under the direction of God). We all knoweth the big ten from The Book of Exodus: don't murder, don't steal, don't covet they neighbour's ox, ass or wife (some choice) etc but verily, some of the others made pretty whacky and entertaining reading. I couldn't possibly list all of them, so I've selected some of the odder ones:

Six days thou shalt do thy work, and on the seventh day thou shalt rest.

Penalty for working on the sabbath – death by stoning. (Exodus, Chapter 23)

Presumably you can't stone anyone upon the seventh day either. That's a kind of work, after all. Actually, this law turned out to be a bit of a break for us Jewish lads. When the Romans first occupied our lands, they tried to make us fight in their army against their enemies. We all refused, saying that we were terribly sorry but we could not possibly carry arms, let alone fight, upon the sabbath. This hacked them off no end, but eventually the whole issue turned out to be more trouble than it was worth, so they let us off.

He that curseth his father, or his mother, shall be surely put to death *(Exodus, Chapter 21)*

(Sorry mum, only joking).

If a man strikes his slave and he or she dies upon the spot, he

must be punished. But he is not to be punished if the slave survives for one day or two, because the slave is his property. *(Exodus, Chap 21)*

This one's a bit daft. I should think that if I was the smitten slave, it would mean precious little difference to me if I died immediately – or at a later date.

Slaves generally get a pretty raw deal round these parts. Thou canst become one in several ways. Firstly, if perchance a Jewish man's a bit hard up (or unscrupulous) he can sell his nipper into slavery, though they need only be in the job for six years before being set free. This, of course, maketh Jewish slaves a lot cheaper to buy than Gentile ones. You can pick up a Jewish slave (in good nick) for between five and ten minas, whereas a Gentile one (who'll be your slave for life), couldst set you back a cool 100.

Some of the folk around these here parts picketh up their slaves (cheap and foreign) from the cash-and-carry at the local seaports, but must circumcise them before they canst be put to work.

If a slave owner is about to die, he can settle his slaves upon his next of kin (like a house, or herd of goats) but, verily, the next of kin, if he's got enough of his own, can sell the 'bequest' back to the slave's relatives for the going rate.

He that smiteth out his manservant's tooth, or his maidservant's tooth; he shall let him go free for his tooth's sake. *(Exodus, Chapter 21)*

Methinks there must have been a host of slaves running upon the fists of their employers.

If an ox has been for some time a vicious animal, and the owner hast been duly warned, but has not kept the animal under control, then the ox must be stoned to death, and the owner stoned to death as well. *(Exodus, Chapter 21)*

If I'd owned this particular cross ox, I'd be sorely tempted to eat him up pretty quickly and buy another.

If the ox gores *(kills)* a slave or slave-girl, its owner must pay thirty shekels of silver to their master — and then stone the ox to death. *(Exodus, Chapter 21)*

Seems rather fair, though I doubteth the average slave would agree.

If a burglar is caught in the act and receives a fatal injury, it is not murder; but if he breaks in after sunrise and receives a fatal injury, then it is murder. (Exodus, Chapter 22)

Warning to all house-breakers: don't break in at night.

When a man has a son who is rebellious and out of control, who does not obey his father or mother, or take heed of them when they punish him, then his father and mother are to lay hold of him and bring him out to the elders of the town at the town gate, and say, 'This son of ours is rebellious and out of control; he will not obey us, he is a wastrel and a drunkard.' Then all the men of the town must stone him to death. *(Deuteronomy, Chapter 21)*

I've heard of severe punishment, but that soundeth a little upon the excessive side. I reckon my brother Jim should take heed.

Thou shalt not suffer a witch to live. *(Exodus, Chapter 22)*

This all pre-supposes that thou wouldst recognize a blinking witch if thou met one.

Thou shalt not seethe *(boil)* a kid in his mother's milk. *(Exodus, Chapter 23)*

I hope he talketh about goats!

Thou must not eat an animal that has died a natural death or has been mauled by wild beasts, thereby making thyself unclean . . . *(Leviticus, Chapter 22)*

79

Could be tricky. How in God's name dost one interview a deceased beast to find out how it died?

A curse shall be on anyone who misdirects or places obstruction in front of a blind man. *(Deuteronomy, Chapter 27)*

I should think so too! That soundeth a dirty rotten trick.

Do not allow two different kinds of animal to mate together. *(Leviticus, Chapter 19)*

I'd be a touch surprised if they'd want to. Imagine the weird beasts thou'd get if they did (See Noah chapter 14)

It is forbidden to cut the hair from your temples or shave the edge of your beards. *(Leviticus, Chapter 19)*

I supposeth that's a career in hairdressing out of the window.

Thou shalt not make unto thee any graven image, or any likeness of any thing that is in the heavens above, or that is in the earth beneath, or that is in the water under the earth. *(Exodus, Chapter 20)*

Bang go my garden gnomes!

Thou shalt not plough thy land with an ass and an ox yolked together. *(Deuteronomy, Chapter 22)*

Good thinking! Thou would, more than likely, end up with curved furrows.

For whosoever man he be that hath a blemish, he shall not approach *(to present the food offerings of the Lord);* **a blind man, or lame, or he that hath a flat nose***(?),* **or anything superfluous***(?)* **Or a man that is broken-footed, or broken-handed, or crook-backed, or a dwarf, or hath a blemish in his eye, or be scurvy or scabbed** *(yuk!)* **or hath his stones** *(testicles)* **broken.** *(Leviticus, Chapter 21)*

Henceforth, I shalt guard my 'stones' with my life.

If a man marrieth a woman but she does not win his favour because he findeth something offensive in her, and he writes her a certificate of divorce, gives it to her and dismisses her, and if, after leaving his house, she goes forth to become the wife of another man, and this second man turns against her and writes a certificate of divorce, gives it to her, and dismisses her, or dies

after making her his wife, then the first husband who had dismissed her is not free to take her as his wife again; for him she has become unclean. *(Deuteronomy, Chapter 24)*

Crikey! Talk about passing the poor soul around! I knoweth a few women who might have a lot to say about that!

If two brothers live together and one of them dies without bearing a son, the wife must go to bed with the brother who is left. If she bears a child, then verily it must carry the dead brother's name. If, perchance, the brother refuses to take her, however, she must go up to him in the presence of the village elders, pull his sandal from off his foot, spit upon his face and declare 'That's what happeneth if you refuse to build up your brother's family'. His family will be then known throughout Israel as 'The House of the Unsandalled Man'. *(Deuteronomy, Chapter 25)*

Bizarre, or what? –

You must not have unequal weights in one's bag – one heavy, one light. Otherwise you are an abomination to the Lord your God. *(Deuteronomy, Chapter 25)*

How very odd. I think the Lord soundeth a touch over-sensitive.

The woman shall not wear that which pertaineth unto a man neither shall a man put on a woman's garment.

I suppose that puts the tin lid on fancy dress parties.

You must not gash yourself in mourning for the dead or tattoo yourselves. *(Leviticus, Chapter 19)*

Shame, I was going to procure an 'I love everyone' tattoo.

So, thou gets the picture, it's all pretty strange stuff. Be warned, however. If, by any chance, you don't obey these, and the multitude of other rules, God told Moses (Leviticus, Chapter 26) that he would send forth sudden terror, wasting disease, recurrent fever and plagues that dim the sight and cause your appetite to fail (which might not be a bad thing for fat folk). On top of that, thine enemies would come and eat all your food. If that didn't do the trick, and you still defied the Lord, he threatened to send wild beasts amongst you to tear your children from you, destroy your cattle, and decrease thy numbers so much that all thy roads are *deserted*, and then make sure all your fruit would be infested by the mole-cricket (and that certainly ain't cricket!).*

Lo, if you still don't heed the rules of God, he said that he wouldst make you eat your sons and daughters (not in one sitting – surely), pile up your corpses on your idols, lay waste your cities, and pursue you with a drawn sword.

*I'LL GIVE YOU 'WHAT'S FOR SUPPER?' YOU **ARE** SUPPER!*

And if that doesn't put you off, you canst expect Egyptian boils, tumours, scabs and severe itching from the soles of your feet to the crown of your head. Every daybreak, he went on, thou wouldst say 'Would God it were sundown,' and every sundown, 'Would God it were daybreak.' You know, it really surpriseth me not, after all that lot.

13th July 13 AD

After some consideration, I've decided to leave all that sort of stuff to the elders in the synagogue. There's no way I want to spend my life checking on such things. Maybe I'll go and swot up on the civil law.

* Sounds bliss!

82

Nazareth's only a weeny village, so in order to check out how civil and criminal law work, I had to go forth to Sepphoris.

When I finally came upon the courtroom, there appeared to be a throng of the most scruffy, sleazy-looking yobbos milling around the entrance to the fine Roman edifice. I cornered one and asked.

'Excuse me sir, but art thou having to appear in court shortly?'

'I dunno mate,' he scowled, 'all depends if I gets lucky.'

'How dost thou mean "gets lucky"?' I enquired in a puzzled manner.

'Depends if I gets a brief,' said he, leering at me with a new-found interest. 'Why, what are you up for?'

'I ain't up for nuffink – I mean – I'm not here for anything,' I replied, still puzzled. 'What about you? Are you not accused of a crime?'

He looked upon me long and hard, and then threw back his head and laughed with a sarcastic guffaw.

'What d'you take me for, you silly twit. I'm a lawyer! I'm tryin' to find some poor mug to defend. All of us 'ere are lawyers. We hang about the courtroom, tryin' to pick up the punters as they come here to be done.'

And it came to pass, as it was getting towards the end of the morning session, the lawyer decided to take a break and sat down upon the ground with a huge wineskin from which he proceeded to drink. I asked him how the whole law business worked and, as there wasn't anything else to do, he spake thus unto me.

Apparently, it all used to be a lot simpler in the olden days. Trials as such were all a bit of a gas, being conducted in the open air at the gates of cities. The verdict was, as like as not, based upon how much the poor sucker in the hot seat couldst come up with, cash-wise, and everyone involved would have a bit of a divvie-out if and when he was let go, or stone the poor geezer to death if he was a bit short of the readies that day.

Lo, ever since the Romans started throwing their considerable weight around, however, the whole operation hath become far more orderly, though no less cruel. Mind you, they hath attempteth to give the poor blighters a fair trial, something unheard of in the past.

The way it worketh is thus. To start with, there is this bloke called a PRAETOR who, when someone is pulled up before him, listeneth to what he or she hath to say in their defence, before deciding upon whether it is even worth going forth to trial at court. Whereupon, if it is what we call a CRIMEN (an offence against religion or the gods), he letteth the local priests or rabbis at'em. If it isn't, or he didn't think there was anything in it for his boys, he letteth the somewhat relieved person go free, without taking even the smallest 'fee'.

The now slightly sozzled lawyer then went forth to explain that if this praetor guy thinketh there is a case to answer, then the accused will go before the judge — usually some high-ranking Roman military prat who hath got a bit too long in the tooth for soldiering.

I asked him how someone manageth to get themselves before this praetor in the first place. Crime in our village, I'm glad to say, is practically non-existent, and most of us wouldnst know where to go if we were nicked.

He then told me that if, say, someone hath a grievance with another; whether it be a dispute over land, goat rustling or pick pocketing, etc; he must get a mate to witness him ordering that person to appear in court. He maketh this official by holding on to the witness's ear when he speaketh. That person then hath to turn up to be heard — it's the law — and that's where the lawyer comes in.

The amount the lawyer chargeth seems a bit hit and miss. He told me it depended how much loot the punter hath. If, perchance, he was a poor farm labourer or skint slave, for instance, he couldst not sting him for much, but lo, if he be lucky enough to pull a merchant or landowner, he couldst sometimes take him for a veritable packet.

But it was when I asked him about punishment that it all sounded a bit hair-raising. I was surprised to learn that, even at this advanced period in the history of mankind, the old eye-for-an-eye principle is still all the rage. The Romans, being the cruel creeps they are, hath long decideth that, if they are to get into the execution business in a big way, they might as well make it into family entertainment. One of the current fads is to dress the guilty party in some fantastic fancy apparel, tie him or her to a post, douse'em in something highly inflammable and then, in front of a happy cheering throng, put a torch to him. If, perchance, they already hath enough human 'fuel' for their fires they wouldst allow some of the stronger male criminals to train within special schools and then join the ranks of gladiators. Unfortunately, it is a touch

heads you lose, tails you also lose. If, fr'instance, the man in question turneth out to be rather fab at the old gladiating, and isn't topped within the first year, he will then be executed anyway which, I should imagine, removeth a little incentive. This is sometimes done by crucifixion (nailing the poor devil upon a wooden cross, and then letting him expire in a slow, sort of lingering way); or by offering him to a load of their fiercest and hungriest beasts, much to the enjoyment of all and sundry.

I had known that, for minor crimes, we Jews often liketh a good bout of the old SCOURGING: that is, smiting the victim thirteen times upon the back and shoulders with a rod. The Romans go one better (or worse), and useth strips of leather with pellets of bone or metal set into the ends – guaranteed, to really mess'em up good.

If they don't fancy killing or disfiguring them, they'll often sell their poor charges into slavery, which requireth them to toil in heavy chains whilst being whipped continually (see very bad work conditions in ancient times). Another Roman trick is to hang their victims up by their hands with heavy weights attached to their feet, so that their toes only barely touched upon the ground (guaranteed to make their arms somewhat achey), or carry a heavy wooden structure, like a huge forked pole, around their necks, while working. If a slave or thief runneth away, he'll be brought back and branded upon his forehead (known as a STIGMA), probably with a return address, just in case they ever escape again.

Another well-loved punishment, is to put sinners to work at the corn grinders upon the treadmill, as a replacement for done-in donkeys, or failing that; as a method of propulsion (with 50 or so colleagues) for the huge ships that tradeth on the high seas.

Suddenly the bell tolled for the recall of the court and my now, totally pissed lawyer friend staggered to his feet and lurched into the midst of the milling throng outside the court house, proclaiming his extremely reasonable charges at the top of his voice.

15th July 13 AD

Verily, as I thought back upon everything that the horrid bloke spake unto me yesterday, I became more and more convinced that the law's about as cruel and corrupt as the folk it's supposed to administer unto. I am, therefore, going to inform Mary, my mother, that verily, it's not for me! I know it says in the Book of Ecclesiastics. **'He that hath the knowledge of the Law shall obtain her wisdom'**, *but from what I've found out within the past few days, I'm not so sure.*

Jesus Enters the Wine Business

The juice of the grape was the standard drink in Jesus's time, being more plentiful than water for most of the year. Children, of course, would drink the juice in its natural state, but adults would take theirs fermented as wine. But the consumption of alcohol as now, was not always in moderation and drunkenness, particularly amongst the male of the species, was a huge problem, even in Nazareth, where our young hero lived.

3rd Janaury 14 AD

Let it be known, I have nothing against those who drink wine, but verily, when they lurch past my window after closing time, singing their silly heads off, blaspheming like centurions and smiting each

other, almost totally daft with their drunkenness, it really getteth my goat. And when they get home, it wouldst appear, they abuse their poor wives and take much advantage of them.

Not only that, but that dreadful excuse for a man that runneth the inn in the village must be making a multitude of shekels at their expense. I know exactly what he buys his wine in for and how much he chargeth. Verily, he rips his brethren off well and truly. I say unto you, if something does not come to pass pretty soon, the whole village will see the wrath of the Lord – and who wouldst blame Him.

5th January 14 AD

I awoke in the middle of the night having thought up this wizard wheeze. What's to stop me getting in on the act? I could go forth and buy the wine direct from the vineyard, shove it in vessels, stick snazzy labels upon them and sell those vessels direct to the multitude at reduced prices. Brilliant! It shall go by the name of Chateau Nazareth.

And, when I make profit from the enterprise, I shall use the money to help the wives and kids of the drunkards. With the Lord's help, I can then adopt Plan B to wean those sinners off the blood of Satan's grape.

14th January 14 AD

This looketh dead promising. With the money I saved from my wages, I went forth and bought enough wine, direct from the growers, to fill maybe two score and ten vessels. I know the scriptures sayeth **'thou shalt not put new wine in old bottles'** but, having only the empties I'd collected by the roadside, I have given them a quick sluice-out and then have filled them to the top. The labels look a bit crude, but I'm sure they'll do. CHATEAU NAZARETH is now a goer.

2nd February 14 AD

Glory be! The stuff is shifting as soon as I can bottle it and verily it would appear, at this rate, that the evil old skinflint, down in the village, will soon be looking for a new business, as it may soon come

to pass that I've a complete monopoly. I think the time cometh soon for Plan B.

9th February 14 AD

Hallelujah, I have them all eating – or should I say – drinking, right out of my hand. The time must be well-nigh to start my scam. I reckoneth that if I dilute the wine just a little bit, the customers will never notice, and the saving, therefore, will allow me more cash for my work amongst the drunkards and their poor families. And when they've got used to that, I can water it down a teensy bit more, and then even a little more still. Tee hee! Not only will the sinners' money be ploughed straight back to those that depend upon them, but I'll also be cutting their foul drunkenness at a stroke. A touch devious, but surely God will agree that, in this case, the end justifieth the means.

17th March 14 AD

How canst this be? They are now drinking over fifty per cent water and nobody hast even made a murmur. Tis brilliant! The village inn is now tottering (and so too the old rogue that runs it) and lo! I'm beginning to notice far less bawdy singing and foul swearing in the street after the hour of darkness. I must take heed, however, as my mum and dad are becoming real suspicious at the number of people that climbeth the back stairs to my off-lic. . . . sorry – bedroom. But fear not! By the time they twiggeth it, I'll have achieved my goal.

21st May 14 AD

This becometh silly. My brethren are now drinking just 20 per cent wine and 80 per cent of the old H_2O and are only just beginning to wonder why it comes to pass that they bowleth home in the evening feeling as right as rain. Not only that, but their women sport far fewer bruises and black eyes, and they are even beginning to get to recognize their own children.

26th May 14 AD

Wouldst thou believe it? I've now got a complete stranglehold on the local wine business. Verily, I'm selling the punters practically coloured water, but they feel so good, they don't seem to mind. On the negative side, I've heard tell, through the grapevine ('scuseth the pun), that all the local wine growers are tearing their hair out as, not only have I become their sole outlet but, needleth to say, I'm no longer buying hardly any of their produce. On top of all that, I'm taking so much water, on my midnight visits to our well, that the women folk runneth out of rope to tie onto the bucket. Verily, everyone's becoming dead suspicious.

31st May 14 AD

Lord! Am I ever going to get murdered if I carry on with this? The natives are sure getting restless. By pure chance, however, there came upon me this day a weird tourist who, after trying my 'wine' said that he might be interested in buying my idea. He told me that, in the far, far distant land from whenst he comes (Perrier, in France), he hath discovered a constant supply of natural spring water that fizzeth, but unfortunately he can't get rid of it, as the French only drink wine.

If truth be told (and verily it must), I don't really mind selling out. I've practically eradicated drunkenness and have united many broken families in the village. On top of all that, I've made enough loot to put a tidy sum away for a day which raineth (and enough wine for a right good bash!). As for the wine business, I really feel that retailing is not for me and, let's faceth it, there's a fair chance I'll never need to go forth and turn wine into water again.

Canst that be what we call 'a result', oh Lord?

Strangely enough, later in his life he did face a similar problem. This time, however, the circumstances were the other way round and came about when Jesus was invited to join his mum at a local wedding in Cana, a few miles up the road. In John Chapter 2, the story goes that, owing to his uncanny ability to get things fixed, he was asked if he could sort out the total lack of booze at the wedding party. After a while, he told them to fill up six huge stone jars with water and – Hey presto – ten minutes later they mysteriously contained a rather fine vintage of delicious red wine. Even Paul Daniels couldn't do that!

Jesus Builds an Ark

One April afternoon, Jesus and his dad were working in the carpentry shop, next to the house, when a strange man came in to see them. Joseph recognized him as old Mr Jehosaphatson, the decidedly odd hermit, who had lived for years up in the hills outside Nazareth. Rumour had it that he'd gone badly bonkers after making a fortune selling horses and camels to the Romans when they moved in force, into Palestine, after Herod's death.

3rd August 14 AD

Dear Diary
I was toiling with Dad this very morning on the cart for that creepy Mr Nathanson, the undertaker, when behold, this strange old guy called Mr Jehosaphatson came in and started babbling in a most odd manner. What a fruit cake!

'Take heed, all you sinners!' he cried. 'Take heed! The end is nigh. We must prepare, for verily the waters will soon overtake the earth and we shall be drowned to death. Take heed of what I say! Oh woe, oh w—'

'Hang fast a mo,' broke in Dad. 'Holdeth thy horses. What in heaven's name art thou rattling on about? This is a carpentry shop, not a blinking synagogue. Pray tell us what we are supposed to do about it? Now slow down and speaketh of what's upon thy mind.'

'Lo, I had a vision, a terrible vision,' he moaned in a quavery voice. 'A vision of death and destruction. Men, women and children floated face down in the flood and every creature, that hitherto walketh or creepeth upon the earth, was belly up — drowned. Oh woe, it's too late to repent. The end is ni—'

'Cool it old man,' said I, 'haven't we heard all this before, Dad? Wasn't there some joker way back who went through the same thing and knocked up some sort of floating hotel for all his rellies, and a host of assorted beasts?'

The cranky old cove seemed a bit psyched-out by this, and mumbled something softly. Then he leaped forth again and half scared the wits out of us.

'Never mind all that,' he screamed. 'I wanteth a new ark and I wanteth it quick. Verily, there's no time to spare. The end is upo—'

'Twisteth not thy knickers,' said Dad. 'I don't know who thou thinks we art, but we're just ordinary carpenters. You know, cupboards, bookshelves, pipe racks, that sort of thing. Thou wanteth a boat-builder.'

'And a loony bin,' I whispered.

'The only boat builder in the area has just sawn off his hand and hath retired,' he raved. 'Thou art the only people I know who couldst possibly build it.'

'Look, I'm terribly sorry,' Dad responded, 'but even if we couldst build you some kind of a boat, we're terribly busy (what a fib!) and it wouldst cost quite a lot of money.'

'Listen,' the old man's voice dropped to a conspiratorial whisper, 'I have loads and loads of cash and I shalt pay you more than extremely well.'

With that he brought forth an old pigskin bag from beneath his coat, and out trickled a small fortune in golden coins (the ones with Caesar's head on) upon the bench.

Dad's eyes opened wide and lo, his manner changed completely. He ushered old Mr Jehosaphatson to a chair and sat him down upon it.

'Ah well, of course,' said father, 'there's no point hanging on to all that money, if thou art simply going to drown with it. Actually, now I remembereth, someone did say we were in for a lot of rain. Let's face it, I suppose tis better to be safe than sorry.'

Blimey! If I hadn'st known better, I could well have thought that my dad was stringing the old geezer along, simply to ease a heap of dosh out of him, but I was well miffed with myself for thinking such unkind thoughts.

'Now let's getteth down to business,' Dad continued. 'What sort of thing didst thou have in mind, sir?' (Notice the 'sir'!)

The old nutter went on to describe the weirdest, over-the-top sounding craft, which resembled a potted version of the one I half remembereth hearing about during scripture lessons. I told Dad that I would go forth, on the morrow, to chat up the rabbis, who might be able to find the bit in the scriptures that describeth the building of the original.

D'YOU THINK NOAH'S ON DRUGS?

4th August 14 AD

I didn't let drop to the old men at the
synagogue why I wanted to know about the ark,
for fear that they would either think, if they didn't
already, that I'd finally lost my marbles or worse, that it might put
the wind up the villagers. Dad and I knew our now precious old client
wasn't right within the head, but there was little point telling them
the whole story.

And lo, eventually, they hit upon the piece right at the beginning
of the Book of Genesis that I desired to read. It turned out to be
a most way-out and fascinating yarn, which I will now endeavour to
retell.

Right; here we goeth!

Once upon an ancient time there was this guy called Noah. Now
Noah was a well known good-guy, at a time when God was hacked
off, to say the very least, with the rest of us humans. Apparently
we'd been a-sinning left, right and centre (and God was well-sorry
He'd ever invented us). The only thing He reckoned He could do was
to wipe the whole lot out and start again. Drastic but effective!

He picked old Noah to be, sort of, commander of operations and
forthwith set about whipping up a huge worldwide flood. God advised

Noah that he'd better look sharp and get building a socking great boat so that he and his immediate family could be saved. Noah's clan wouldst be in charge of begatting (bible speak for breeding) like mad when it was all over, in order to start a brand-spanking-new human race again.

Nice one, thought Noah (even if his poor old Mrs wasn't that thrilled) but, unfortunately, that was only the good news. The bad news was that God had (rather meanly, I think) decided to zap all the beasts as well, so poor Noah had also to find room for two (a boy and girl) of every single creature, be it mammal, bird, reptile or insect in order that they too could begat like crazy after their boat trip. Apparently, God wasn't too bothered about fish, for fairly obvious reasons.*

Notwithstanding, and to cut a long story short, Noah and his three sons, set about knocking up this ginormous floating, wooden apartment-block-cum-zoo on many floors in, you'll never believe this, their back yard. Their nosy neighbours must have thought them well potty, as one doesn't generally go in for building huge boats miles from any water. But poor Noah couldn't split on his old mate,

---

* Fish don't seem to mind water too much.

God, by telling them what was soon coming to pass, so had to put up with all the mickey taking.

Eventually they finished this huge zoo-boat and hung around waiting for all the animals who, having been given fairly precise directions from God, started to pitch up (in pairs) from out of nowhere. Everything from pandas to penguins, rabbits to roosters and adders to aardvarks climbed, hopped or slithered up the gangplank where one of Noah's sons, Ham (I bet he was popular with the pigs!) ticked 'em off before they went into their new home. Shem, his other son acted as bell-boy and showed them forth, once within, to their new quarters, while Japheth, the youngest son, asked them all (as best he could) what they usually liked for tea.

No sooner were they all within, when the first plop of rain fell on old Noah's bald pate. Verily, it was the 7th February by all accounts.

'Looketh like rain,' Noah said, rather stupidly.

'Sure does daddy,' giggled his boys who, up to this time, had been humouring the old chap (after all, he was nigh on 600 years old).

Anyway, they laughed upon the other side of their faces when, later, more filthy black clouds rolled over from the east and even larger plops of rain started to fall. Soon the drips turned to drizzle, the drizzle turned to a shower, and the shower turned into a torrent of solid H$_2$O. And lo, they laughed on yet another side of their faces(?) when it poured down for 40 days and 40 nights, without

a break. Little puddles turned into ponds, ponds turned into lakes and the lakes turned into mighty oceans (which eventually joined up). By the time it eased up there was not a sign of life, save for the odd corpse, or the odd chair, cart or wheelbarrow, floating by (please don't ask what happened to all the other boats in the world).

On the 17th July (dead precise they were in those days) the flood started to subside, and by October the ark, which by this time smelled like a pig's lavatory, became lodged on the very peak of Mount Ararat which looked well daft.

And it had come to pass, by this time, that all the sons' wives were with child (let's face it, there was precious little else to do for five months, bobbing around on a boat). But worst, when the sons went forth to the animals' quarters, there was a right chaos. Jeez! If you were to take the rabbit room, for instance, it must have been heaving with a mega-multitude (bunnies only having a three week pregnancy).

Actually, I've got this really wild theory. What if, by accident, Noah's lads had carelessly left a few of the rooms unlocked? Some of the sharper beasts could have got out and done a bit of inter-begatting.

Wouldn'st that account for all those oddballs like stripey horses (zebras), spotty lions (leopards), beaky beavers (platypuses-or is that platypi?) or rhinos (who looketh like a mixture of blinking everything)? Just an idea!

Anyway, when they all piled off the ark, the humans and beasts all went forth upon their different ways to set up homes. All except Noah (and his long-suffering Mrs) who, as it sayeth in the scriptures, started a vineyard and then spent the rest of his life (Noah died aged 950) drunk as a skunk and naked. The punch line to the whole story was that God made a promise to Noah that He would never send a flood again, which must have come as a bit of a relief to all the animals as well. In order to remind them of His promise, He invented the rainbow, which He told them would switch on every time it stopped raining.

Verily, it says in The Book of Genesis:

'My bow I set in the clouds
to be a sign of the covenant
between myself and the earth
When I bring clouds over the earth
the rainbow will appear in the clouds.'

5th August 14 AD

When I related the story to my folks over breakfast, this morning, Dad nearly fell off his chair with mirth.

'How d'you fancy that, Mother?' he asked. 'A nice little cruise for six months upon a homemade house-boat with a multitude of smelly beasts?'

'I'll give thou arks,' she yelled. 'Thou needn't think you're going to drag me upon your floating zoo. I've heard nothing so ridiculous. And as far as starting the human race again. Lord above, as if I haven't got enough to do without going upon stupid boat trips. You tell him Jesus!'

We all had a right giggle about it, and after breakfast Dad and I went up to see the old man in his cave. Luckily, it turned out that all he wanted was something slightly more modest, just large enough to keep (or should I say 'save') him, his cat, parrot and three cows.

It took about three months to build his craft. Jesus's dad was right all along, he certainly wasn't any good at boats, and the thing looked as if it had been designed by a committee that had fallen out with each other. No way would it have ever floated. The old hermit loved it, however, and moved in straightaway. He soon became a feature of great interest in the neighbourhood, and people came from afar to gawp at this dotty old geezer living in a haphazard boat halfway up a blinking mountain.

As we know (from God's promise), there never was going to be another flood, but Joseph never had the heart to tell him (and business was business after all), so old Mr Jehosaphatson lived on his 'ark-ling' for the remainder of his days. Every morning, he went on the deck and searched the skies for rain clouds. Still, nobody could ever say the old nutter wasn't prepared!

Jesus the Fixer

One evening, Jesus was sitting round the supper table with his family when his dad mentioned that one of his old acquaintances from the village, called Nathan, had got himself into serious debt over a get-rich-quick scam, and that the guy to whom he owed all the money (his employer), would have him thrown into his own personal dungeons when he discovered the loss. Jesus, it turned out, was at school with Nathan's son Joshua (a real bully), and realized full well what would become of his family if the worst happened to his father.

4th October 14 AD

Dear Diary

Every time I looketh across at poor Joshua in class I wonder what will befall him. 'Tis true he's a rude, aggressive pin-head, but I'm sure there are reasons for that and, after all, there has to be good in everyone. Verily, if it comes to pass that his old man does get banged up, he and his mother and sisters will be thrown into deep distress and will have to live upon paltry handouts from the villagers. Lo, I've tried to ask Josh if there is anything I can do to help, but his replies were so rude that they'd burn a hole in the papyrus if I were to try and write them down.

But I couldn't get his poor father off my mind, so tonight I questioned Dad once more over supper. This time he spake much more.

'It turneth out,' he said, 'that Joshua's dad, Nathan, met this bloke who'd just come from way up north, where he'd heard that there was soon to be a plague of boils raging throughout the land.'

(In those days, plagues were two-a-shekel, as God sent them whenever he was a bit vexed with the human race.)

Mum's hand went straight to her mouth, but Dad continued.

'Apparently, these huge boils covereth the sufferer from head to foot and stay with them for the remainder of their severely-shortened lives. Anyway, while this stranger was in Syria, he said he'd come upon an ancient apothecary who claimed to have concocted a cure for this approaching plague, but didn't have the wherewithal to finance making it in large quantities. The stranger then told Nathan that he'd personally paid to have a score or so bottles of the highly expensive potion made up just in case it caught up with him on his travels. The plague, he said, spread like wild-fire and would smite Galilee within a couple of weeks. There was, it wouldst appear, a fortune to be made by anyone with enough money to invest in supplies of this miracle potion.' Dad scowled to himself, took another draught of his wine (which none of us were allowed to touch), wiped his mouth and continued. 'Anyway, Nathan apparently licked his lips with greed upon hearing this, but was, notwithstanding, severely sceptical. After all, he thought, this guy couldst be making it all up, and he certainly was not the sort to be taken in by a two-bit stranger with a cock-and-camel tale like that, so he showed the guy the door. By pure coincidence, however, just at that moment, another man staggered in, swathed in bandages, a-wailing and a-gnashing his teeth. He said he had just been travelling up from the south, when lo, he'd suddenly broken out in horrid lumps. Thereupon, he unwrapped some of the bandages and there, all over his head and neck, were the most disgusting, greeny-yellow, weeping boils that gave him the visage of some sort of alien from Hades.'

Mother gasped with shock and rushed yonder into the kitchen to throw her recently-downed dinner . . . up.

Dad continued with a hint of a grin.

'Anyhow, this poor guy with the boils looked really a-feared when the stranger told him of the plague but, luckily, the stranger seemed genuinely sympathetic towards his plight. He offered the afflicted man a swig from a sample bottle that he just happened to have within his cloak. The man took a deep draught and then, by all accounts, put his hands to his face and, in even more agony, rushed

out the back of the bar, where he couldst be heard ripping at the bandages and screaming in anguish.

'Fifteen minutes later he staggered back, amazed and totally without raiment but, and it had to be said although not exactly a fair sight, without a single mark upon his head or body.' Dad then paused while we all looked totally agog.

'Lo,' he continued, 'Joshua's father was gobsmacked and totally convinced, realizing that, when the plague did smite Galilee, he would be daft not to get in on the action. He told the stranger not to tell another soul and agreed to meet him there the following day with as much cash as he could lay his hands upon.

'Now Nathan (Joshua's dad) was the manservant of one of the wealthiest landowners and merchants in Galilee, a certain Hiram Cohenson, and he, and he only, knew where the old miser kept his vast fortune. He also knew that he counted his fortune every three months, upon the quarter day.

'That night, so the story goeth, he crept down to the vaults and "borrowed" two thousand silver talents knowing that within weeks, and well before counting day, he'd be able to pay his master back with great ease.'

Mum returned to the room, a little shaken, but anxious to hear the remainder of the yarn.

'Anyway,' Dad persevered, 'on the morrow, Nathan met the stranger who, sure enough, had the sample bottles upon him, and a deed of purchase for the remainder. Indeed, Nathan seemed rather

104

encouraged by the fact that he appeared relatively unimpressed by the vast sum that he'd come up with. The stranger simply shrugged and said that if that was all he could raise, so be it. He would go forthwith to the apothecary and would return within one week, with enough supplies to be ready for whenst the plague struck.

'But lo, that was over a month ago,' Dad added, as he got deeper into the story.

'Go on, go on,' we clamoured

'Well, it appears that poor Joshua's greedy but gullible father waited and waited ... and waited but, as you might have guessed, the strange man was never to be seen again nor, as it happened, was the guy who was cured of the boils. To make things worse, he met some merchants from the south who said that, though their camel train travelled hither and thither, throughout many lands, for months and months, they had never heard tell of a plague of any description.

Just to put the tin lid upon it, the landlord of the inn, after clearing up the store room out the back, found, stuffed behind some old wine skins, an armful of bandages and what looked like a load of artificial boils wrapped up amongst them. Verily, it seemed Nathan, had been stitched up rotten.'

'What came to pass when his boss found the money gone?' we demanded in chorus, upon the edge of our seats.

'We've yet to find out,' concluded Dad, sitting back with that, let-that-be-a-lesson-to-you-all expression that we all knew so well.

18th November 14 AD

Ah well, it's now over six weeks since the money was 'borrowed' and, sure enough, when old Mr Cohenson came to do his quarterly count-up, last week, he spotted the deficit instantly and knew straightaway that it was Nathan that had nicked the lolly. Despite much pleading and grovelling, and promising to repay it throughout the rest of his life, old Hiram threw him down into his deepest dungeon, and rumour hath it, threw away the key.

All through the last couple of days, I just couldn't rid myself of the idea of the wretched man languishing in a dark, dank subterranean cell, with no one for company but rats. So, after much toing and froing within my mind, I decided to go visit the old miser Cohenson in his huge mansion, just to see if I couldst change his mind.

20th November 14 AD

With much fear and trepidation, I dragged myself out of Nazareth, by the Nain road and, after several miles, came upon the front gates of old Mr Cohenson's mighty estate. A guard, armed to the teeth, asked my business and then disappeared within, for what seemed like an eternity. Eventually he returned and, grudgingly, ushered me to follow. As I walked through the courtyard, I noticed the latest new-fangled water clock, or clepsydrae (invented by the Greeks), the first that I had ever seen, but seeing as I couldn't tell the time it was of fat use to me.

The house was enormous, and built in the Roman fashion; all marble columns, statues and stuff, and my footsteps echoed like drops in a mighty well as I trailed through long corridors towards Mr Cohenson's private rooms. I tapped gently upon the massive door and lo, a wizened old servant directed me into a vast room with no furniture, save a huge marble table, behind which there sat an ancient, even more wizened, man slumped over piles of papers. I walked with great foreboding up to the table and stood for maybe five minutes before he, without looking up, croaked in a low-pitched voice, that resounded and rebounded round the room: 'Well?'

'Good morrow, sir,' I squeaked, the sound almost refusing to issue forth from my mouth. 'I'm terribly sorry to disturb you, but I come on behalf of my schoolfriend's father.'

With this, the ancient man's head emerged tortoise-like from his

106

shoulders and he viewed me through deeply sunken, bloodshot eyes.
'And who, pray, do I have the privilege of addressing?' he asked in a
sarcastic, thou-must-be-the-lowest-form-of-life manner.

'Jesus of Nazareth at your ser . . .' I started, but my voice trailed
away as his piercing gaze drilled right into my very soul.

'And who, wouldst thou be talking about?' he demanded, with more
menace than King Herod on a BAD day.

'Your personal manservant, Nathan, your honour; he whom you
currently keep within your cells.'

'And will do until his very bones rot in hell,' he added with a leering venom that sent shivers right down my back. 'What couldst thou possibly say about that slug, that abomination, that boil on the backside of humanity, that could possibly make things any better?'

'Ah yes,' I stumbled. 'I canst understand your displeasure with this gentlemen, sir, but it was about a plague of boils that I....'

'Boils? Boils? I'll give thou boils,' he screeched. 'Don't speak unto me about boils. What hast thou come for?'

'I was wondering if you might find it in your heart to forgive him,' I whispered in a voice that slid beneath his desk and cowered by his feet.

'FORGIVE HIM? ME – FORGIVE HIM?' he screeched. 'May he go down to the very bowels of hell, his entrails devoured by the foulest vermin, his liver roasted to a crisp and fought over by demons before I ever forgive him.'

'I realize thou feelest not well disposed towards him,' I replied gently, aware that my interview was going that well, 'but the Lord hath said, "**Thou shalt forgive them that trespass against you.**" so I thought that you might.'

The old man suddenly sat upright and said in a thin but menacing voice. 'If you're going to preach morality at me, you young whippersnapper, God also said, "**An eye for an eye, a tooth for a tooth.**" ' He then looketh well pleased with himself.

' "**But whoever shall smite thee on thy cheek, turn to him the other,**" ' I parried cautiously.

' "**To me belongeth vengeance, and recompense: their foot shall** slide in due time,"' he snapped back, eyes a-blazing, obviously not used to being challenged.

'"Love thine enemies. Bless them which despitefuly use you,"' I ventured, my voice rising slightly.

Then there passed a long pause, during which the old man hobbled up and down mopping his brow and tearing at his hair. Suddenly he turned and pointed straight at me, freezing my very blood.

'"And they shall know my vengeance upon them with furious rebukes,"' he screamed deliriously, verily believing it was game, set and match.

I hesitated for a second and then spake in my calmest, steadiest voice, '"Forgive us our debts, as we may forgive our debtors."'

The old man slumped upon his chair, looking truly beaten, and then slowly looked up to me with a fearful stare that could have stripped paint from a door. Just as I thought he was going to call his guards and have me sent assunder to join Nathan in the dungeons, a gurgling noise came from within him that sounded like water, coming up from a newly struck well. It got louder and louder and, verily, I thought he was about to have a heart attack. Suddenly, as the weird noise reached a crescendo, he threw back his head and laughed a laugh, the volume of which, I never before heard. It ricocheted round and round the room bringing forth all the guards and servants to the doorway to watch dumbfounded at the spectacle of their master amused for the first time in living memory.

He guffawed uncontrollably for nigh on fifteen minutes and lo, as suddenly as he had begun, he stopped and fixed me with the same menacing, icy grimace as before.

'What is it that thou actually want?' he wheezed, exhausted by his own laughter.

I cleared my throat, looked straight at him and said, in a calm strong voice. 'I would like you to forgive thy manservant, release him from his debts, and reinstate him in his job.'

He looked upon me for a full ten minutes, but, though trembling like a jelly,* I broke not eye-to-eye contact.

'I will do as you wish,' he answered eventually, 'but woe betide him if he should ever do ill again. Now go forth from my house, young Jesus of Nazareth. I've heard all about you.' And with that he hobbled grumpily to the far side of the room and out to his private rooms.

30th November 14 AD

The news of Joshua's father's surprise release hath rocketed round Nazareth and the whole district like the most virilent virus in only a couple of days. Nobody knoweth my involvement in it, and that suiteth me fine. Old Cohenson's servants had, apparently, spoken of some weirdo who had an enormous effect upon their boss but, luckily, none of them kneweth who I was.

The most amazing thing about this whole business was that, when I returned to school, Joshua (the man's son) still looked well fed up, which to be totally honest, he hadn't, all the time his dad was locked up. After asking around, it appeareth that his father was more of a bully than Joshua was (always the case) and his whole family had been relieved and even a bit delighted when he was put inside for ever.

'If I ever get my hands on the interfering twerp who talked old Cohenson into releasing that old so-and-so, I'll tear him limb from limb,' Joshua scowled to an assembled throng. 'Why can't folk mind their own blasted business?'

I came home with heavy heart tonight.

1st December 14 AD

Over the breaking of fast this morning, Dad related an amazing addition to the Nathan saga. It appears that just before he was

* Not invented yet.

110

apprehended by old Cohenson, he had grudgingly lent five shekels (a paltry sum) to one of the ne'er do-wells that drink in the local inn.

A couple of days after his release, Joshua's dad was in the bar when this chap walked in. Nathan demanded his money to be repaid then and there, but the guy, who was still on hard times, said he hadn't got it.

Nathan, by all accounts, then beat the poor devil black and blue and threatened to slay him if he didn't have his money within twenty-four hours. Nice eh?

When I came to bed tonight I realized that, due to my do-gooding, a whole family hath been made miserable once more, and a poor chap was in fear of his very life.

I obviously had to UNDO the wonderful 'good' that I had done earlier. . . .

But how, oh Lord, but how?

2nd December 14 AD

I decided that after school I'd face the music again and risk old Mr Cohenson's ridicule. I went forth to the estate and was surprised to come upon the gates wide open and a large 'Visitors Welcome' sign. As I walked through the corridors of the mansion, I was greeted by happy grinning staff playing various games with a multitude of noisy, scruffy children. They said that the old man had been expecting me, and laughed and patted my back.

As I was shown into his huge office, the old man leaped upon his feet and welcomed me joyfully with open arms.

'Welcome, my boy, welcome,' cried the old man, as he hugged me warmly. 'I'm so glad thou camest, I've been wanting to speak with you.'

'About what?' I enquired nervously. 'I think when thou hearest what I've got to say thou might not be that thrilled.'

'I think I know thy news,' he laughed. 'One of my guards was within the inn when Nathan behaved so disgracefully.'

'Have you thrown him back in your dungeons,' I asked sadly.

'Better than that,' he chortled. 'I have banished him from Galilee. If he ever returneth, he shalt be locked away for the rest of his days.'

Before I was able to ask the next question, he continued. 'And I sent forth a messenger to his family and have agreed to pay unto them what I wouldst have paid unto him, for the rest of their days.'

'But why?' I asked incredulously.

'You showed me that revenge is no use to anyone. Your bravery was a great lesson to me. I also decided to distribute the great part of my vast wealth amongst the poor, and throw open my house to all.'

'Nice one, Mr Cohenson,' I replied softly. 'Thank you.'

'Not at all, young Jesus, it is I that shouldst thank you. After all, "It is easier for a camel to go through the eye of a needle than for a rich man to enter the kingdom of God." '

' "If thou will be perfect, sell that thou hast, and give to the poor," ' *I replied with a loud giggle.*

His expression clouded and, just as I thought he was going to explode. Trust me to blow it. Suddenly he roared with laughter, threw his arms around me again and sent out for a huge and sumptuous tea.

Jesus later used this parable (described in Matthew) when lecturing his disciples. In this new version, however, it was a king who was owed 10,000 talents by one of his subjects. He, also, showed great compassion and released the grovelling man from his debt. When, however, the wretch mercilessly punished a man who owed him a much smaller amount, the king had him tortured mercilessly until the debt to him was paid in full. Ah well. That's royalty for you!

Jesus Plans a Surprise

It doesn't take the greatest biblical historian to realize that eating in Jesus's time was severely limited compared to these days of relative plenty. There were no shops or restaurants, never mind Waitrose or Sainsbury's (with vast camel parks). Even old McDonald, the patron saint of fast food (and farms), had not blessed the world with his awe-inspiring presence. Most of what was consumed, apart from the wheat needed for bread, was grown or reared in the back yard, and had to be prepared by the lady of the house, while hubby was out a-toiling in the fields (or in Jesus's dad's case, knocking things up in his carpentry shop). Goats and sheep had to be milked; vegetables, such as they were, had to be pulled out, cleaned and prepared; and the wheat ground for the bread (as in 'give-us-our-daily'), before being baked in the home oven. As there was a severe shortage of fridges and freezers, all the food had to be eaten real quick, owing to the intense eastern heat. You couldn't even go to the larder and grab a tin of Baked Beans. Canning, as such, wasn't invented until 1812.

The average daily meal, eaten in the evening, usually consisted of a small range of seasonal vegetables, flavoured by home-grown herbs, cooked over a fire (often of wood and donkey-dung) and always eaten with the sort of flat unleavened bread that looked like swollen frisbees (and tasted like 'em). The Galileans were big on fruit, and most households grew grapes, figs, dates, pomegranates and mulberries.

Fish was fairly plentiful but, as mentioned before, would go bad as soon as you looked at it, so it would usually be salted, dried in the sun and stored for later. Meat was a luxury, fowl being more useful for their eggs, and goats, sheep and cows for udder things like milk and cheese. It would, however, be eaten for special celebrations – birthdays, religious bashes unless you had a good supply of prodigal sons (and fatted calves) due home.

The diet, therefore, compared to the junk we eat today, was mostly vegetarian and dead healthy. Life threatening conditions, like choked arteries, were unheard of (possibly because they hadn't been discovered yet).

Meals were leisurely affairs, as no one had to jump up to watch *Neighbours* or *Top of the Pops*, or rush out to go to the movies or the pub. Families, unlike today, would then generally go to bed quite early (and get up even earlier).

Jesus had always fancied himself as a bit of a cook and, despite the later fiasco of the loaves and fishes (see page 148), relished the opportunity to prepare simple food for his folks. Jewish people, then and now, had a whole set of rules related to clean and unclean food. One of Jesus's great problems was that he was a little shaky on what food could be eaten and what couldn't so, as you can imagine, he got a bit bogged down when ordering the nosh.

We join his diary as he prepares for a surprise dinner party for Mum and Dad's wedding anniversary. He'd never really done any fancy cooking before, so didn't know quite where to start, but he certainly wanted it to be a meal to remember.

Dear Diary,

And it came to pass, just as I was about to go forth unto the village to purchase the extra grub for the forthcoming feast, it came upon me that I'd better nip to the synagogue to check in The Book of Leviticus what Moses had actually told the Israelites what they could or couldn't eat. I knew it wasn't going to be a doddle, but didn't envisage it becoming a nightmare. I asked the old elders (or is it eld olders?) to read the relevant scriptures to me. I knew I was becoming a bit of a pain but it simply had to be done if I didn't want to invoke the wrath of either my parents, or worse, him that must be obeyed, the Lord.

In the beginning, they started by saying that God would permit the eating of any of the big animals that hath cloven feet and chew the cud; which is bad news for sheeps, cows, deer etc, but good news for anyone into mutton, beef or venison. Anything that only hath cloven feet or only chews the cud, however, is simply not on, and is unclean. This certainly prohibiteth the eating of pigs, as pigs don't have cloven feet but chew the cud (and who'd want to eat those filthy creatures anyway); and, I suppose, rabbits and hares, even though they both chew cud (and look delicious).

'OK,' I said, 'how's about camel? We'll haveth camel. Can't I buy a few camel chops and shove 'em upon the barbie?'

'Oh no!' chorused the elders. 'Although the camel has a cloven hoof, it will eat just about anything (except cud), which makes it also unclean.'

This really gave me the hump but, notwithstanding, I thought I was getting the picture. Later on the elders read some more from Leviticus:

'The carcasses of every beast that divideth the hoof, and is not cloven footed, nor cheweth the cud, are unclean unto you: everyone that touches them shall be unclean.'

or:

'You are to regard as unclean, all four-footed wild animals that walk on flat paws.'

(Which I suppose ruleth out bear-becues, dogs (hot), lions or pandas or pussy cats.)

All this was beginning to make my brain hurt.

'What about fishes?' I enquired, now wishing I'd bought my parental wrinklies an ordinary present and forgotten the whole feast idea.

One of the rabbis continued to read:

'These ye shall eat of all that are in the waters, whatsoever hath fins and scales that are in the waters, in the sea, and in the rivers, them ye shall eat.'

Now we're getting somewhere, I thought. I naturally supposed that meant that all manner of sea and river creatures were OK, but then he went on:

> 'And all them that hath not fins and scales in the seas, and in the river, of all that move in the waters, and of any living thing that is in the waters, they shall be an abomination to you.'

Hang on a mo! Abomination? That's a little O.T.T., I pondered, and also a bit of a blow, as I rather fancied serving up some nice squid cooked in red wine and garlic, or some delicious lobsters or crab; or failing that a nice prawn cocktail. Even an eel or three. Oh well, I supposed I could cope.

'How's about the birds of the air?' I asked the elders.

'Thou must be very careful,' said another of the ancient men as he dived back into Leviticus. 'You can't eat any old birds, you know. For a start, you're not allowed to eat eagles, ospreys, vultures, kites, ravens, cuckoos, owls, storks, herons, cormorants, lapwings or bats.' (Holy batburgers!)

Now I reckon that would be a bit of a relief, as I wouldn't touch most of 'em anyway. (By the way, I could have sworn a bat ain't a bird.)

'And no swans or pelicans,' he added sagely.

'That's a shame,' I blurted out, 'I would have thought swan and pelican pie would be rather fab.'

The old men looked down their noses and pretended that they hadn't heard.

By now I thought I was really getting the picture, but then the old man read on:

> 'Of all fowls that creep, going upon all fours, shall be an abomination to you.'

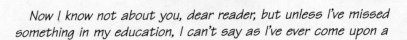

Now I know not about you, dear reader, but unless I've missed something in my education, I can't say as I've ever come upon a *four-legged bird. Then he read on:*

'Yet may you eat of every flying, creeping things that goeth upon all fours, which have legs above their feet *(how can you have feet with no legs?)*, to leap with all upon the earth.'

Short of the winged horse Pegasus (of which there's only one), I'm sure I can't think what they mean. It really was (and is) quite bizarre.

Then, believeth it or not, a tiny little rabbi piped up: 'It's fine to eat locusts, grasshoppers and beetles.'

Wow!!! I wonder how Mum and Dad wouldst react to that?

Fortunately, they forbade me to cook weasels, mice, tortoises (tortoi?), ferrets, chameleons (whatever colour) and lizards. Unfortunately, snails were also off, which was a bit of a drag, as I was going to whip up a few escargots en croute (snails in pastry) – which I'd seen on a French cookery tablet – as one of the starters.

'And if any beast, of which you may eat, die, he that toucheth the carcass thereof shall be unclean until the evening.'

'Now hold fast a minute,' I said, 'isn't it fairly usual for something you're eating to die, or at least not feel very well.'

The elders simply looked at each other and then at the sky as if to say, 'What hath we got here, oh Lord?'

Finally they told me that in Leviticus God forbade the eating of anything that creepeth upon its belly – presumably with no legs (that'll be a relief for tax-collectors!).

To be perfectly honest (which I must always be), I'm now even more confused as to what's clean or unclean. P'raps I'll send out for a take-away. Oh pooh! I've just remembered. They haven't been invented yet!!

Jesus and the First Supper

Despite all the problems of what his brethren could and couldn't eat, Jesus decided go ahead with the surprise feast.

The day finally arrived for Joseph and Mary's surprise anniversary party. Both were, luckily, to be out all day while Jesus helped by his brother Jim (in theory) prepared his first ever big bash. To be fair, Jesus had been down to the local market to see if there was anything he could buy them as an ordinary present, but all they had were the usual dresses from India, shirts from Cilicia, veils from Arabia, sandals from Laodicea, baskets and jugs from Sidon or poodles from France (only joking). A wonderful feast, he thought, would be remembered for the rest of their lives.

Anyway, after all that toing and froing with the rabbis, about what was or wasn't OK to eat, Jesus had decided that he wouldn't do anything too adventurous, preferring the more traditional route – roasting a whole sheep which would be the centrepiece of the meal. Mum and Dad, being guests of honour, would traditionally be served the tail of the sheep as it was reckoned to be (despite where it came from) the most tasty bit.

As a starter, he'd decided to have grasshoppers barbecued and served with honey (to take the bitterness away). This was a great delicacy, believe it or not, in ancient Palestine. For days, he'd had all the little kids in the village darting about the fields collecting the grasshoppers, and now had a huge stone jar practically hopping itself, due to its bouncy inmates.

After the grasshoppers, he'd settled on quail and partridges (chickens had only just been invented and weren't that common). Next, to go with the lamb, he would have beans, onions, leeks and garlic, which he would cook in oil, and little cucumbers (gherkins) to be eaten raw. Huge wicker baskets would be filled with fruit and placed on a long, low trestle table that was to be laid out under the olive trees.

119

Jim was in charge of the drinks (see dangerous delegations). He would have to spice the various wines, prepare the delicious drinking yoghurts for the ladies, and squeeze fresh pomegranate juice (no Coke yet) for the many kids that would be there.

Typical of Jesus, over the last week or so, he had invited a very weird assortment of guests. As well as his parents' close friends and relatives, he had asked a few of the tramps and destitute people he'd met as he passed between the rellies' houses. He even invited a couple of the unsavoury low-lifes and estate agents who hung around the village inn, as they looked as if they could use a good square meal. All of them were highly suspicious, of course, but as everyone, by now, expected Jesus to do whacky things, they were inclined to believe him and, after all, a free meal was a free meal.

15th September 15 AD

Dear Diary

Today started off slightly shakily. Mum and Dad set forth at daybreak upon their journey to see Uncle Jeremiah, who's been very poorly for the last few weeks. Lo, as soon as they were gone, I leaped from my mattress and threw my clothes on. I had only one day to prepare the surprise feast so that it would be ready upon their return. I quickly dragged brother Jim out of bed, as his first job was to slay one of our sheep and hang it up to drain the blood from its body (kosher style). I would have done the slaying, but I have never killed anything in my life before and, besides, I knew also that Jim wouldn't bat an eyelid (unless it was someone else's).

120

And it came to pass, just as I was about to start preparing the vegetables, the door burst open and one of our huge grown-up rams burst through the door with Jim hanging upon its horns with a knife betwixt his teeth. The odd couple tore round the kitchen, sending all

the baskets of vegetables and fruit flying. As I scrabbled on the floor, trying to gather them up, the frantic pair knocked over the huge grasshopper pot. They, hardly believing their luck, leaped forth and began hopping about with great gusto. I dived for the door just as the ram (plus Jim) flew back out, and slammed it shut — so preventing the grasshoppers from becoming even more liberated. For the next two hours I leaped and dived, tripped and sprawled, and cursed and cheered until, one by one, I recaptured all the varmints and returned them to their temporary residence.

Horrid noises came from without and suddenly Jim, bloodied from head to foot, staggered through the door with an evil smile upon his face.

'Jeeesus,' he exclaimed, 'that was some battle. I was beginning to wonder whether it was going to be him or me for supper tonight! Didst thou get them blasted grasshoppers back into the pot?'

I carried on with the vegetables, pretending I hadn't heard him. I'm the sort of person who hath a conscience when I pull up a vegetable or cracketh an egg, so you can imagine how I felt about ex-rams.

'Couldst thou start preparing the drinks, Jim?' I asked politely. 'Midday's nearly upon us and we've no time to lose.'

'Sure I will broth,' he yelled cheerily, licking his lips ominously.

Lo, I was suddenly stricken with a deep sense of foreboding.

As the day progressed, things on my side passed relatively smoothly. Naomi, the vast girl (with the small, black moustache), came round from next door and helped with some of the difficult bits, like preparing the various sweetmeats for later and putting flowers and decorations upon the table outside. Jim, unfortunately, proved to be rather too good a wine taster, and by mid-afternoon was lurching round the back yard hither and thither, harassing the flocking sheep, or making eyes at Naomi (which verily proved his drunkenness).

Just as I was putting the finishing touches to the preparations, I heard a commotion outside. Lo, when I opened the door, I saw a multitude of the most ragged and unsavoury people that I'd ever seen in one place, milling towards our house. Every unfortunate that I'd invited had obviously mentioned to all their mates that there was a free bash at Jesus's house and the few had turned into three score or more.

Jim thought it was a gas and, seeing as he knew most of them, invited them in and showed them to the booze. I warned them that the food was off limits until my parents arrived, but that worried them little (as long as the alcohol lasted).

Verily, after about an hour, our house looked like a war zone, with filthy, scruffy varmints draped everywhere – singing, swearing and blaspheming at the tops of their coarse voices. Jim, of course, was right in their midst, claiming it was the bestest party he'd ever been to.

When the proper guests arrived, dressed in their finery, they only had to get to the front gate to realize what was coming to pass and, muttering that they'd always found our branch of the family a bit off the wall, assumed that we'd finally lost the plot, and simply turned round and returned from whence they came.

By the time I saw Mum and Dad trudging wearily up the front path, the fracas had reached its high (or low) point and verily, I thought, it resembled Sodom and Gomorrah on a BAD day (see Genesis, Chapter 14).

'And what in Hades' name goeth on here,' yelled Dad as he reached the door. 'It looks like Sodom and Gomorrah on a BAD day,'

'Great minds thinketh alike' I nearly replied . . . but thought better of it.

'Look father, it's not what it appears,' I started.

'I'll give thou "not what it appears" – it's worse than it appears!'

screamed Mother, peering within at the drunken orgy. 'Really Jesus, we thought better of you. Who art these dreadful people?'

'Ah well, Mother, to be truthful (which I always am) I knoweth not exactly. Please let me explain.'

I told the old folk all about the surprise party and how I'd invited a few extra because I'd felt sorry for them. Gradually they quietened down and, one by one, Dad and I chucked all the uninvited guests (including my brother) out upon their ears. This was far easier than one might imagine as, by this time, most of them were practically horizontal and incapable of resistance.

I was then sent forth to rush round and re-invite all the guests, which tooketh the best part of a couple of hours. Most of them returned (albeit warily) and lo, we had the most wonderful celebration. Unfortunately, by the end, Dad became a bit the worst for wear and mother flung him out too.

The Gospel According to Luke tells of when Jesus, in later life, recounted the story of the rich and powerful man who planned a huge bash to celebrate his birthday. Jesus turned the story about face by saying that the guy, rather foolishly, prepared a huge feast first and *then* invited all his friends. Without exception, they all told him that they were doing something else (which I think sounds perfectly fair), but it made him well mad.

Now anyone else would have cancelled, but not this guy. He simply sent his servants out to collect all the low-life they could find to fill up his table.

The moral of this tale seemed to be that very often good, religious Jews missed out on God's kingdom, while God Himself welcomed all and sundry, and was perfectly capable of accepting the very people they despised.

Jesus and the Bad Samaritan

Although the towns and villages in Palestine were fairly safe when Jesus was a lad, it was a different story when you had to travel between them. The chances of being robbed and/or mugged and/or raped and/or murdered (and/or worse) were pretty strong, and it was decidedly dodgy to travel alone by day or night. After the run-in with the school bully, however, Jesus, although not realizing that it was God that had saved his bacon (being kosher), reckoned he was fairly indestructible, even bionic. He didn't think twice about travelling, unaccompanied, wherever and whenever he pleased.

Every year, at around Passover (the fab festival in spring that reminded the Jews of God's rescue of their people from Egypt), the Davidsons, now a two-donkey family, would load up their animals and trudge off towards Jerusalem (where the poor long-suffering Jews were now under the thumb of the Romans), along with thousands of others to pay homage to the Lord their Saviour. All good Jews, in those days, were expected to live within ninety days journey of the city (no cars, planes or trains, remember) and were required to pay half a shekel per annum towards the upkeep of the main temple.

Jesus's brother Jim, who hated all this religious stuff, would stay and look after the various beasts (and drink himself into a stupor).

As he got older Jesus, who'd always been a bit of a loner, sometimes went on ahead of his parents and spent a bit of time in and around the many temples in Jerusalem. Let's join our hero a couple of days from home.

18th February 16 AD

Dear Diary
What a day! What a day! I'm completely wiped out. My feet feel

like they're worn to veritable stumps after all that walking. Mind you, it wouldn't have been half so bad if I hadn't had to retrace my steps several leagues.

It happened like this. There I was, sauntering along with the dreadful Jezebel (her of the personal hygiene problems), minding mine own business, not that far outside Sebaste on the road to Jerusalem, when I came upon this poor geezer who'd been held up by a bunch of right rough boys. He'd been severely worked over and had been relieved of everything save his underpants — not a pretty sight I might add! Lo, when I questioned him, he turned out to be a Samaritan, a tribe that us Jews have never seen eye to eye with (owing to their annoying habit of thinking that they are the bees knees and the only folk that God really likes). Verily, they were the lot that split from the main Judaic stem way back, when all the joyful Jews were on their return from Babylon to Jerusalem.

Anyway, I digress. This Samaritan told me he'd been on his way from Jerusalem to Sebaste on business (he sold camel accessories), when these three hoodlums leaped from the midst of the shadows and relieved him of all his merchandise, money and even his camel, which they'd used as the get-away vehicle. He then told how he'd been completely ignored by several pilgrims who passed by, and that the last one, who had crossed onto the other side of the road to avoid any dealings with him, had been an actual man of God (nice, eh?).

Now, I've never gone a bundle on Samaritans either – a cocky lot to tell the truth – but, notwithstanding, thought the least I couldst do was tend to his cuts and bruises, and get him to somewhere where he could rest up for a bit. I mean, it's the least one canst do – is it not?

'Why doest thou this for me?' he asked. 'I thought you mainline Jews liked us as much as we like you lot.'

'Look,' I replied, 'I know it's not much of a compliment to you, but I'd help anyone in this state – even Romans.'

'Verily, thou must have been in the sun too long,' he groaned. 'Who the hell art thou, anyway? And what, pray, is in it for you? Don't think you'll get anything for thy trouble – it's all been nicked.'

'Jesus of Nazareth, at your service,' I answered, 'and, thank the Lord, my rewards will be in a better place than this. Now, where hurteth it most, mate?'

'In my blasted wallet,' he cried, 'the devils have cleaned me out completely! Honestly, I know not what the world cometh to. I blameth the parents.'

I beseeched him to rest while I patched him up as best I could, and then slung him over Jezebel. I wondered what wouldst kill him first, his wounds or Jezebel's foul odour.

I suddenly remembered passing a small, run-down inn called the Traveller's Rest Camel-tel some way back, so I wearily retraced my steps with my strange cargo straddling my foul donkey. We arrived just before sunset, and there I spake unto the decrepit old innkeeper about my poorly charge.

126

'Wouldst thou look after this poor merchant, kind landlord?' I asked. 'I came upon him three leagues yonder and, verily, he was well poorly, having been done over good and proper.'

As I spake, I looked towards the public bar and saw three dreadful looking young dead-beats who, leering at my poor friend, seemed to be drunk out of their skulls and spending money like it goeth out of fashion.

'Blimey,' spake the foul old landlord, 'thou must be joking! He looks like a wretched Samaritan. It's more than my reputation's worth to have one of them within my respectable establishment. Anyway, you said he'd been robbed so who, might I venture to ask, is going to pick up the bill? This ain't a blasted charity home, you know, or a hospital come to that.'

Everyone knew that the inns upon the main trade routes were often little more than foul drinking houses and brothels, but there seemed no choice. I told the old skinflint that I'd cough up for a few days board and lodging, and wouldst call back on my return from Jerusalem to settle any further expense he might have run up. The old man grumbled, but as soon as he caught wind of hard dosh, brightened up and helped the wounded Samaritan inside. The Samaritan looked upon me as if I was completely off my trolley and, verily, seemed more frightened of me than the landlord and all those ruffians put together.

24th February 16 AD

Jezebel and I finally came upon Jerusalem this afternoon and spent an interesting couple of hours being right tourists: strolling through the crowded streets while making for the southern edge of the city. It was here that we would find the house of my Auntie Sarah. Me, Mum and Dad always stayed within her home as it saved us spending a fortune at an inn. We all knew how tight my father was.

And lo, if I happened to speak with anyone, I kept it under my cloak that I came from Galilee, as we Galileans were regarded as real oiks by the smart city folk. Luckily, I'd swotted up on a bit of Greek at school so did not seem too out of place with the largely Greek-speaking Jerusalemers.

Jerusalem's verily a magnificent place, built upon two hills and dominated by the bad old ex-King Herod's flash palace, which is faced with cream marble and encrusted with precious stones and lashings of gold. I say bad old Herod, but he sure kneweth how to build cities — his temple, for instance, was to die for (which he did). There's also a magnificent Roman amphitheatre where the less-than-magnificent occupying Romans indulge their favourite sports — chariot racing, gladiator fighting, or watching their pet lions and tigers dining (usually upon us Jews).

Indeed, everywhere you look within Jerusalem, Roman soldiers sprawl around in their short skirts and soppy tin hats (the ones with the brushes on the top), drinking and womanizing, and picking upon anyone they feel might make a decent snack for their beasts.

FANCY COMING OUT TO EAT— OR SHOULD I SAY—<u>BE EATEN</u>, WITH US?

They even race each other through the streets, lounging upon litters carried by four black slaves (eight-leg drive?).*

Lo, we've had to putteth up with these bullies for over three score years and ten now throughout most of which Herod, the creep they put in as pretend King, 'ruled'. When he'd passed on fourteen years ago, however, things went from bad to far, far worse, as those ruddy Romans, thinking things were getting a touch slack, sent in a large, lusty legion of real thugs to crack down upon the inhabitants even more. They now act like a kind of secret police, picking upon Jews at random, safe in the knowledge that it is out of the question for us to try to defend ourselves. In truth, the only function we Jews now seem to fulfil, is paying taxes, building their socking great palaces for them, and providing pet food.

Anyway, back to the yarn. Mum and Dad were well tired when they finally turned up a day or so later but, when they had rested, had a great social time, meeting up with a host of their friends from past years.

My old lady and Auntie Sarah seemed to spend most of their time sitting around, sipping gallons of mint tea, and gossiping upon the events of the past year. Who'd done what, with and to whom, both in the big city and in our village.

Dad, meantime, discussed politics and business with his old chums at one or the other of the local bars. Precious little worship seems to come to pass, but let's faceth it, it's the only holiday they ever get, so I'm sure God won't begrudge them a couple of weeks off.

30th February 16 AD

A day to remember – or perhaps try to forget. I'd set out for home with Dad's other donkey, old Nebuchadnezza, early yesterday, (Jezebel, though horrid, was slightly stronger and could carry the extra junk my old folks always seem to collect in Jerusalem) and we were heading homeward upon the long road to Sebaste. As we trudged along, I noticed a plume of smoke rising from a point in the distance. As we got closer, it turned out to be a burned-out building. Lo, it was the remains of the very camel-tel where I'd left the injured Samaritan.

* In modern Jerusalem, the negresses that control the vending of roasted peanuts are descended from those very slaves. They are easily recognizable by their flamboyant clothing, three-legged stools and red hot braziers (ouch!).

Sitting in front, with his head in his hands, wailing and screaming the most terrible blasphemies, was the same old horrid landlord. He looked upon me with a desolate expression, but obviously recognized me not.

I then spake unto him: 'What cometh to pass, old man? How come your gaff is burned to the ground?'

'Oh woe is me! Woe is me! You may well ask. Verily I am ruined,' he sobbed, wringing his hands and rending his clothes.

'But what cometh to pass?' I asked again. I was about to enquire where my sick Samaritan was, when he butted in.

'Oh woe is me.' Several days ago some weird do-gooder brought in an injured Samaritan and left the so-and-so with me to care for, pending his return. When he had recovered, the creep robbed me of all my money, nicked my eldest (and prettiest) daughter and, as a parting gift, set fire to my home and business. All this, after I gave him the refuge of my establishment. Such ingratitude!'

I must admit, it did seemed a touch thankless. I was just about to tell him that I was that very person who'd left the Samaritan in his care when, in the nick of time, I thought better of it and swallowed my words.

'Pray tell me what was this stranger, who left you this rogue, like?' I enquired, trying to sound as casual as poss.

'How canst I remember, after all that has befallen me,' he cried. 'All I know is that he had the filthiest, smelliest, ugliest donkey in all Judaea. I'd know it anywhere. If I ever clap eyes or nose on the beastly beast or its do-gooding owner, I'll get my three sons to tear him asunder, mark my words.'

It suddenly dawned upon me that it had been his three lewd lads who'd beaten up and robbed the poor, unfortunate Samaritan in the first place and, therefore, it must have been them that I'd seen killing themselves (for a change) laughing in the bar that eventide. The wicked old man had been in on it all the time and the robbing of defenceless travellers was obviously a lucrative family sideline. I bet a thousand shekels that the Samaritan had sussed the whole scam and had, therefore, acted accordingly.

'Well,' spake I, with a wobbly smile, 'I'll certainly keep an eye out for this guy with the disgusting donkey and make sure he returns to settle with you.'

I hoped, and silently prayed to God, that he didn't recognize Jezebel when she passed by with the old folk.

The old man just scowled, spat on the ground, and continued alternately cursing and wailing. Verily I thought, as the old donkey and I continued on our journey, '"**He that sows thistles shall reap prickles.**"'

As you probably know, Jesus, later in life, in his famous Sermon on the Mount, went on, to convert this story in to a well-known parable. In this version, however, the Samaritan became the good guy, saving an injured man by the roadside (when no one else would), taking him to an inn, and finally coming back to settle the bill. The moral of the story is of course, that you shouldn't judge people by their race or creed.

Jesus Teaches Saturday School

Jesus was nineteen and becoming well versed in the scriptures. Despite sometimes being a pain in the . . .synagogue, the rabbis were pleased with his knowledge and thought he might be a good choice to replace old Mrs Isaacson who had just retired from running the village Saturday school. Jesus was very nervous to say the least but, believing it was God's wish, agreed to give it a go.

3rd July 16 AD

Dear Diary

Oh dear, oh Lord, what hast I let myself into? I've just found out that there will be at least thirty kids, who rangeth between four and nine years of age. But worst than that, they will have in their midst the dreaded Elijahson twins, who have a reputation for being the noisiest young hooligans for leagues around.

For the last couple of evenings, I have prepared my lesson down at the synagogue. I decided I would tell my little flock about my great, great (x100) Uncle Moses's early life 1200 years ago, as it's a good yarn and, with God's will, should keep the little blighters' attention.

Most of the text I've copied down from the Book of Exodus, but I'll try to simplify it for the little darlings and explain anything they have problems with.

4th July 16 AD

Thank God that's over! Verily, if I never see another nipper again it will be far too soon. The lesson came to pass at two o'clock this afternoon and, as far as I can remember, went something like this: 'Good afternoon, children,' I said in the most authoritative voice that

I could muster, 'and how art you all today?'

Total silence greeted me until one of the older lads piped up. He, because he was a dead ringer for the kid sitting next to him, I assumed to be an Elijahson twin.

'Who asketh?'

'My name's Jesus,' I replied cautiously, 'and I've come to tell you all about Moses and his—'

'Moses who?' yelled the other twin, who was trying to pick his nose with his brother's finger.

'I'm afraid I know not his other name, but truly it really isn't that import—' I struggled, beginning to feel my authority threatened.

'Get on with it,' cried the first one, who I now know as Joram, 'we've all got homes to go to, you know.'

'Once upon a time, a long, long time ago,' I began. 'Ther—'

'We've heard thith one,' interrupted a little girl casually who, hitherto, had been busy showing her tummy button to the little boy next to her. 'Is thith going to be the one about that thilly man who built a thilly boat to keep his thilly petth in?'

'No, it'th – sorry – it's not actually that one,' I spake in a strangled – but still calm – voice. Lo, I was trying to hang onto some sort of control.

'We want that one! We want that one!' they all clamoured, jumping up and down as one.

I ignored them and carried on. 'Once upon a time, in a land called Egypt there lived a lot of Israelites who'd settled there many years before. They were good, righteous people who toiled hard, tending their flocks and worshipping the Lord.'

Two little girls jumped up and said that they wanted to go to the toilet. I accompanied them outside and when we returned, the rest of the kids, who'd been charging round the room, began to settle down. So far so good, I thought.

'But lo, there came a wicked Pharaoh (which was an Egyptian sort of king),' I continued, 'who hated foreigners—'

'What's foreigners?' chirped up Jesham, Joram's twin brother, taking a rest from bashing the kid in front with his slate.

'They are people from other lands who happen to be in your country,' I explained.

All the kids then started fighting each other about who was foreign and who was not, until pandemonium reigned. I quietened them down again and tried to resume.

'Anyway, this wicked king declared there were too many Israelites in his land and decreed that they should be made to work so hard, making bricks and building mighty temples and palaces, that they would never be strong enough to be any threat to his own people. This didn't really work, so he decreed that every new-born Israelite boy should be chucked into the River Nile and drowned.'

Upon this, all the girls started laughing and taunting the boys, who promptly began smiting them and pulling their hair. I waded into the midst of them, yanking them apart and forcing the boys to sit on one side and the girls on the other.

'Now, one couple,' I continued, 'called Jochebed and Amram had such a beautiful son . . .'

'Like me,' piped up Joram, standing up and beating his chest.

'. . . that they decided to hide him.'

'Where?' shouted Jesham. 'How couldst you hide a baby like Joram?'

Joram then leapt upon his brother, and hit him over the head with the doll of the little girl sitting nearby, who began to cry.

Ignoring them, I continued.

'They hid the baby in a wicker basket in the bulrushes, at the water's edge, and his big sister Miriam was put in charge of minding him.'

'Why didn't it sink?' cried a little girl. 'Why didn't all the water pour through the holes and drown him?'

Girls are always so blasted practical.

'Because they smothered it with tar,' I answered, making it up as I went along.

'What, the baby?' laughed the girl.

I ignored her.

'Then what happened?' they yelled as one, pretending to cover each other with tar, and then make as if their hands stuck to everything they touched.

'It came to pass, one day, that the Pharaoh's daughter was strolling by the river with a few of her slaves when she heard a baby's cry.'

'Why can't we have slaves?' yelled Joram. 'We want slaves, we want slaves!' they all joined in. Poor Jeremiah, the smallest boy, was dragged round the room as the newly recruited slave of the twins. 'Why can't we all have slaves?' they screamed again.

'Because you can't!' I shouted, beginning to get cross. 'Now shut your mouths and listen! Anyway,' I continued, realizing I was in danger of losing my cool, 'one of the slaves brought the little boy to her mistress who, supposing it was an Israelite, took pity on him and summoned Miriam (the kid's sister) who was lurking within the rushes. The princess then asked who the nipper belonged to, and when Miriam told her, she sent forth for their mother.'

Most of the smaller kids were now becoming drowsy and were lying about sucking their thumbs.

'She then ordered Jochebed (the mother) to bring him up normally until he was older, then to bring him to the palace from whence

135

she would treat him as HER son.'

'I wouldn't like it if my mummy gave me to some rotten old princess when I'm older,' said one of the quieter little boys, beginning to cry at the very thought.

'We would,' yelled the twins as one, 'think of all the toys and money we'd have.'

'And we could have hundreds of slaves to boss around,' yelled Joram, pulling the hair of Jeremiah, his very own slave.

I quietened this new debate and moved on.

'Jochebed, little Moses's real mum, took good care of her baby, telling him that God had saved him from a sure death.'

'God who?' laughed Jesham, but I chose once more to ignore him.

One of the little girls then came up and asked me to do up her sandals. Suddenly the whole class had loose sandals, and it took me a full ten minutes to get them back to their places.

'Now where was I?' I asked. 'Ah yes, Jochebed continued to bring her son up well and, just as he was due to go to the palace and his new mum, she whispered that God would one day help him deliver all his people from the bonds of slavery.'

'Crikey, I wouldn't want to be saved from being a prince,' muttered Joram, beginning to get a bit bored and restless. 'Can't we have a better story?'

136

'OK, to cut a long story short,' I continued, 'Moses (as he was now called) grew up as an Egyptian prince, eating fine Egyptian food, wearing fine Egyptian clothes, and driving everywhere in the latest, snazzy sports-chariot. But, lo, he never forgot that he was really an Israelite, and that his miserable people were still awaiting a leader to save them.'

One day, while out a-cruising in his new chariot, he happened upon one of the Egyptians beating an Israelite slave to death – as was their habit. He leaped down and promptly did the same to the bully, burying him under the soft sand so that no one would know.'

'What did he do with the dead Israelite?' asked one of the little girls annoyingly.

'I suppose he buried him as well,' I replied patiently.

'That's not fair,' she retorted. 'The bully should have buried him – he killed him.'

'How couldst he bury him – stupid,' the girl next to her broke in. 'He was already dead. Dead people can't do nuffink.'

'They can too,' shouted the first little girl, pulling the leg off the other's toy rabbit. 'They can go around haunting people, or being angels – so there!'

A huge argument then broke out about what dead people couldst or couldnst do, so I had to wade in, yet again, and separate them. Verily, I was beginning to wish I'd never started this blasted story but, notwithstanding, I persevered.

'Anyway, someone had seen Moses killing and burying the bully, and grassed to the Pharaoh, who was jolly cross. Thereupon, he threatened to have Moses slain.

'What happened then?' They all cried. 'Did the king do him in?'

'No children,' I replied, 'Moses escaped deep into the countryside of Midian, shedding all his finery, and seeking work as a freelance goatherd.'

'Did he become the Israelite's leader like God promised?' asked one of the little boys.

'No, I'm afraid the Israelites rejected him as well,' I added, dreading their reaction.

'What a stupid story!' one of the twins shouted. 'He should have stayed being a prince – minding his own business. It serveth him right!'

But all the little girls felt sorry for Moses and asked me what came about next.

'Well,' I continued, 'one day Moses was sitting by a well, minding his own business, when seven pretty maidens came forth to water their father's goats.'

'Was that so that they'd grow?' hooted one of the twins.

'No, you twit,' I responded good humouredly, 'watering means giving them something to drink. Anyway, just as the girls were bringing forth the water to the top of the well, some shabby shepherds came upon them and tried to frighten them away (as water was scarce). Moses promptly saw the intruders off, and when the girls later told their dad what he'd done, he ordered them to go back to the well and invite him back for supper.'

'Did their dad like him?' a little girl asked.

'Well, I imagine so,' I replied. 'Verily, he must have done, as he gave him Zipporah, his prettiest daughter for a wife.'

'Blimey,' said Jesham, 'not only does he get a free meal, but he also gets a girl for "afters". Nice one!'

I chose to ignore this remark too, and continued.

'The wicked Pharaoh eventually died and no doubt went right down to the hot place, so God thought it about time that the Israelites got their act together to break free. He decided to have a little chat with Moses, who was by now in the goatherding business,

looking after his new father-in-law's flock.'

'How didst He speak with him?' the kids asked.

'Ah well! This is where it becometh a bit weird,' I replied. All the children leant forward, opened their eyes wide, and went silent.

'One fine day, when Moses grazed his goats upon the side of Mount Horeb, he came upon this bush that appeared to be burning. This of course was odd enough but when after half an hour of watching the flames, he realized that the bush wasn't actually getting any smaller and appeared not to be affected by the flames, it all became odder still.'

'That's stupid,' yelled a little boy. 'How can anything burn without disappearing?'

I dreaded the next bit. 'Then,' I continued, 'just as Moses was about to leave, the bush spake unto him.'

The children all looked at each other with open mouths and then fell about in peals of raucous laughter.

'Did it ask him the time?' squealed Jesham, jumping up and down.

'Did it ask him for a drink of water?' joined in Joram, pretending to squirt water at his twin brother.

'No, it did not,' I continued, trying to speak over the uproar of mirth from all the kids, 'The bush told him it was actually God (in bush form), and that He had chosen Moses to go forth to the new Pharaoh in Egypt to ask if he couldst take all His people to a promised land of milk and honey.'

139

But by now all the boys were leaping about being burning bushes, terrifying the girls, who tore round the room screaming at the tops of their voices.

I promptly picked up my books and walked out, but no one seemed to notice. I really think that I'm not cut out for the teaching business.

Jesus Finds Out

Joseph and his wife Mary were becoming more and more worried. Their wonderful son was now a man and about to quit his teenage years. Despite all the 'encouragement' from his mother to become either a doctor or lawyer, Jesus had shown little or no interest. Joseph had always secretly wanted him to become a carpenter and take over the family business but, although talented and conscientious, his son's heart was never really into wood. Indeed, his forays into the real world had usually been disastrous. His attempts at being a fisherman were short-lived owing to the whacky whale incident (see chapter 9), and as for the wine trade, though it turned out to be profitable, it could have got him into deep trouble as wine-watering was a federal offence in those days.

His parents realized that he had been spending more and more time reading the scriptures and talking to his real father (God), and that his true vocation had to be to preach the word. On top of all that, the people in the village and even further afield were beginning to realize that the carpenter's lad from Nazareth was something very special. Nobody could find in him a single weakness, as he was always courteous, attentive and seemed to mean what he said. Nothing was ever too much trouble and he would try to help everyone, be they rich or poor. The lads had come to realize the futility of trying to bully him, and the lasses had long given up any chance of 'pulling' our handsome, witty hero, contenting themselves with swooning secretly and just enjoying his presence whenever possible.

But it was time for his parents to spill the beans and tell him of all the events surrounding his extraordinary birth. He now must know that he really was the boy chosen by God to save the world. A bit of a tall order for an ordinary Thursday night, after a supper of goat stew and dumplings.

141

24th December 16 AD

Dear Diary

    Phew! I've just got to bed after the most extraordinary conversation I've ever had with my parents. There we were, sitting around the table after supper, when Mum started.

    'Jesus, my darling boy,' she began in a frighteningly serious voice, "tis your birthday on the morrow, and we have something to tell unto you that will change the course of your life completely.'

    I must have looked upon her rather blankly.

    'What's come to pass, Mum? Don't tell me I'm about to get some terrible hereditary disease. Come to mention it, I've been feeling a touch dicky of late.'

    'No, you silly boy – sorry – man, it's nothing horrible, in fact it's totally wonderful,' she said, glancing upon Joseph for help.

    'Gosh! Did my ticket in the Jerusalem lottery come up? Am I to be rich?'

    'In one sense, extremely rich,' broke in Joseph, 'but not in the way thou art thinking.'

    I then looked upon him rather blankly.

    'Come on then, you two – cut to the plot. What's this all about?'

    'Well, you knowest how you've often noted that all your relatives suddenly go silent when you ask of your birth,' said Pa. I nodded

slowly, eyes wide open, 'Well, there's a very good reason, and thy mother will now relate the true story.'

Mum glowered at Dad and then shrugged, resignedly, as if to accept that, tricky as it might be, she really was the only person that could do the job. She swallowed hard and made herself as comfortable as possible.

She began her tale by telling me that it all began way back yonder, when she was engaged to marry Dad. There she'd been, sitting at home, minding her own business, doing a bit of sewing, when this light appeared at the door and forthwith turned into an angel. Mum had never been a drinker, so took this apparition more seriously than most.

This angel, who went by the name of Gabriel, spake unto my mum, and told her that she was going to have a son, and that he wouldst be a sort of a king and the direct descendant of King David. More than that, he would be a famous prophet and save everyone from a dreadful fate. At first she told him that he'd gone to the wrong house as, verily, she was not even married yet. He assured her, however, that she was the one he'd come to visit and that, as a bonus, as twas a bit of a shock, she wouldn't have to carry the nipper for the normal nine months, but could take delivery in three. My mum, of course, felt very honoured (it's not every day that thou gets to be mother of the saviour of the world) but was, notwithstanding, a touch concerned about a) what her fiancée Joseph wouldst make of it, and b) what the neighbours would say.

Now Dad was looking forward to marrying his Mary (and the rest!), and was not at all jolly when his bride-to-be told him; not only that she 'expecteth', but that it was an angel of the Lord that had actually 'organized' it. Lets face it, it could have been the best line ever, in the whole history of excuses for accidental pregnancies. Apparently, my dad was so miffed that he even threatened to break off the marriage (and who canst blame him?).

As luck wouldst have it, however, the old man had a dream that night in which God told him to keep his hair on, as Mary fibbeth not. He then went forth to tell Dad to call the brat (that's me folks!) JESUS, and to bring me up as his own son, even though he (God) was my proper dad. The marriage was on again.

Mum said there was a good deal of a-nudging and a-winking in the village, as she was well-chubby by the time she went up the aisle to be wed. (Actually, I'd have thought that that blinking angel if he had any sense would've given my old lady a twelve month pregnancy, so's no one wouldst be any the wiser.)

143

And lo, it came to pass, just before I was due to make my debut,
Mum and Dad had to set forth on a long journey to Dad's (as I
still call him) home town to register in the census which the Emperor
Augustus had ordered to suss out how many people he could sting
tax-wise.

Poor old Mum, who was about to drop, was bundled up on Dad's
donkey and off they went to Bethlehem where King David, Pa's far
distant ancestor, had started out from.

Now, as thou canst imagine, there were hosts of David's ancestors,
so when Mary and Joe got there, the tiny town was chock-a-block
with people, all milling around trying to get rooms within the only
inn.

Poor old Mum and Dad were apparently amongst the last to arrive
and only managed to find a run down stable to kip in (actually, I
wouldn't have been at all surprised if Dad's meaness had got the
better of him). My mother, always known for her amazing timing,
suddenly realized that the three months were upon her and that
yours truly was actually about to put forth an appearance.

Dad took over the story while Mum partook of a well-earned drink
(non-alcoholic – of course!).

Verily, it was one heck of a night, he said. Firstly, he'd had to
deliver me, which was quite an experience for someone who'd only
ever delivered an assortment of wooden commisions before. Not
only that, but every five minutes there'd be someone knocking upon
the stable door, claiming they'd been drawn by this huge star which
was apparently hanging over the flipping roof. By morning, he went
on, twas sheer pandemonium, with everyone tripping over each other
trying to get a peep of me (I canst barely believe it).

There were shepherds (with their noisy sheep), a multitude of
Davidsons who'd been trying to sleep in the adjoining inn, but had
been awoken by all the toing and froing. Added to that, there were
all the animals that had been resident in the first place, who kept
mooing and ee-awing whilst trying to eat the straw that I was
attempting to get some kip upon.

On top of all that, there suddenly appeared, from out of nowhere,
these three guys upon camels, who claimed they were not only dead
wise but also kings from yonder distant lands. They, apparently, left
three presents – one of gold, one of frankincense, and one of myrrh
(but no cuddly toys!).

MYRRH! Hang on a mo! At this point, I stopped Dad and asked
if that was the same myrrh that he'd given to me when I was doing
my vetting. He nodded slowly and then added sadly that they were

also the same wise men that my cretinous cousin Joab (see Chapter 2) had shooed away upon my thirteenth, coming-of-age, party.

Throughout the night, Mum and Dad continued the story. I heard all about that horrid Herod who, upon hearing about the birth of this super-brat (me??) that was to be King of the Jews, attempted to find me and do me in; and all about my parent's flight to Egypt to save my little life.

Verily, by the time I went to my bed my head was a-spinning. All those funny little, inconsequential things that had happened throughout my childhood were suddenly explained: my fascination with the scriptures; my lack of fascination with girls; my inability to hurt anyone or fight back if I was hurt and, most of all, my burning desire to tell everyone I meet how fab God (whom I now know as my real father) was.

1st January 17 AD

Well, what a shock that all turned out to be. Verily, it's one thing finding out that thy Dad's not really thy Dad (and that my surname should be Godson), but to hear that thou art the one chosen to be the King of the Jews is a different matter. A bit of a responsibility methinks. But, suddenly everything's clear. I must waste no time and begin pursuing my true calling, which is to spread the word of the Lord to all who wilt listen (and even those that won't!). Verily, I really feel the time is nigh to try proper public speaking. I've done bits and pieces down at the synagogue, but it's time to have a go at the big time.

Mind you, oh Lord, it's all very well having these big ideas rolling around within my head, but what's the point when no one heareth? Trouble is, I really know not what must be done to get anyone to come hither and listen.

2nd January 17 AD

Praise the Lord, for I think I've got it! Think BIG!! That's the answer. A scheme of perfection. How come I didn't think of it before? Indeed, if I want people to come and witness my proclamations, I must go forth with much haste and enter into the world of marketing and self-promotion. Verily, to get a real multitude, I must cast the message widely – that is – ADVERTISE. I've tried word of mouth but that didn't work. I've now thought of an extra draw to get those bums upon seats (if I had any seats).

I reckon that if I offer a goodly meal, while they listen to me a-rabbiting on, it might ring the right bell – especially if I make it free. But I need to find a way of buying the grub in bulk. If you're willing, oh Lord, I can use the rest of the profits that I made on the great wine scam.

10th January 17 AD

Well, it's all set that must be set. I've stuck posters on a myriad of vertical surfaces for miles around. Both Dad's donkeys carry smart sandwich-boards proclaiming me as 'THE ONE AND ONLY JESUS OF NAZARETH' and I have tipped the guy who yells out all the prayers and stuff down the synagogue, to slip in a quick shout for me.

I shall fence off a bit of the Mount of Olives, so that a couple of my gang (the junior disciples) can go forth as marshals, while dear Naomi, from next door, disheth out all the grub. I've ordered loads of loaves and practically all the fishes from Friday morning's catch at the harbour. If the punters want anything more fancy it's tough.

My script — or should I say scripture — is all but licked into shape and I've run through it quickly with Mum, who always has quite a goodly ear on that sort of thing.

11th January 17 AD

The sun hath risen on the big day. I went forth early and fenced the mount. Ephraim and Elijah know what they must do. Naomi's laying out all the nosh upon a load of bed sheets that she's borrowed from *around the village. Tomorrow I should have the chance to enlighten the multitude as to where we've all been going wrong and, with the Lord's good grace, kick off my career as a public speaker.*

12th January 17 AD

What a fiasco! There I was, clothed in a white sheet, standing upon the top of the mount with three thousand loaves and barbecued fish spread out in the hot sun to welcome the host and, guess what? Only five turneth up. Heaven above knows what one hath to do to get listened to! That's the last time I try to save five thousand mortal souls and feed them at the same time. They can bring their own picnic next time!

Little did Jesus know, however, that three of the punters that did turn up were very old and very, very wise. Yes, you've guessed it! They were the three kings from the orient in heavy disguise, who'd been gleaning information all through his teenage years. They were over-awed with Jesus's masterly speech and let it be known throughout the lands they travelled through that 'the chosen one' was now good and ready to save his people.

Just to finish the story. In your Bible, Luke, Chapter 9, there's a description of the time, much later, when Jesus, now a bit of a star, had at least five thousand loyal followers sat round waiting for his latest pearls of wisdom. This time, he didn't have a bean to spend on food to feed the punters, and when his poor disciples informed him that all they could beg or borrow were five loaves and three fishes, he realized they were in a bit of a tight spot. Jesus then, so the story goes, told them that the Lord would provide. He asked them to start dividing up the fish and rolls to see just how far they'd go. The disciples, of course, thought their guv'nor had been out in the sun a little too long but, being the loyal lads they were, carried out his orders to the letter. They couldn't believe it, but the more they divided and subdivided the food, the more there seemed to be, until the very last customer was served. When they came to tidy up afterwards, there were enough scraps to fill twelve baskets.

Jesus Leaves Home

So there we have it. Jesus was now a proper grown up and knew, at last, what a very special chap he was and had always been. He also knew that his happy days in Nazareth were numbered as he must spread his 'new' father's word as far and wide as possible, in order to save the world from the slippery path it was going down. He realized it wasn't going to take five minutes, and would be ages before people took him seriously, and so he was resigned to the lonely and often frustrating few years ahead.

There's very little record of where he went and what he got up to, until nearly ten years later, when the New Testament takes up the incredible story of the simple carpenter's lad from Nazareth who lived and eventually died to help his (ungrateful) fellow man.